BURT —
YOU'VE BEEN
A PATRON, SUPPER
+ FRIEND —
WE'LL ALWAYS TAKE
CARE OF EACH OTHER —

GARY

What others have said about Sanctuary

I am honored to have been chosen to comment on your beautiful book and I take that responsibility very seriously. As a Sanctuary member and as your friend, I cannot thank you enough from my heart for what you have done for me and those that I love. Having been a member of Sanctuary for many years, the techniques illustrated in this book seem quite normal to me and to the many people I have sent to the real-life Max. The openness and the excitement of living the wondrous life made possible by Sanctuary is the most glorious gift that anyone could ever receive.

I bless you, Max, knowing that Sanctuary will become a reality available to all, because that is where I live in my heart, right now, thanks to you.

With Love and Thanks

Linda Gray, actress,
Goodwill Ambassador on Women's Issues
to the United Nations

The discoveries of "Max" have been and are fascinating and compelling to me. However, there is an enormous difference to be found between the principles of Sanctuary and other theories; in Sanctuary an immediate "proof" can be seen. There are many examples of the benefits of the techniques illustrated in this book which could be cited by members of our family and our friends. Quite simply, we have never before enjoyed such healthy, energetic, creative years, nor had such a sense of well-being and peace of mind as we have since being beneficiaries of energetic balancing.

If you are interested in a healthier, more focused and creative life, you will find this book to be one of the most important and enlightening experiences of your life. If you join Sanctuary, I know it will be one of the most beneficial experiences of your life.

Lalo Schifrin, musician, composer, conductor

"Sanctuary" is a wonderful book describing a new way of viewing human well-being and consciousness from the latest perspective of subtle energy. By tapping into this knowledge, incredible amounts of detailed information about the status of our well-being, our hereditary energy, our strengths and weaknesses, as well as our potential for healing, can all be quickly ascertained.

The examples presented in this book are based upon real people whose lives have been transformed by a radical new spiritual technology of energetic evaluation and balancing that promises to forever change the way we think about well-being and human potential. Seemingly incredible, the stories behind the fiction are real. *Sanctuary: The Path to Consciousness*, though fictional in nature, is about a real place where we can discover the true nature of dysfunction in our lives and the ways that we may better achieve well-being and inner balance. It is also a story of hope for those individuals with problems and inner imbalances that have persisted despite their best efforts. This book points the way towards an energetic understanding of human existence, leading to new paths of insight and transformation that can greatly benefit all of humanity. I highly recommend that everyone read this book and join Sanctuary.

Dr. Richard Gerber, MD author of
Vibrational Medicine:
New choices for Healing Ourselves
(Bear & Co., Santa Fe, NM, 1988)

It was 1993, and I was in big trouble. After 3 months, 3 hospital stays, exploratory surgery, 24-hour nurses and a staff of 9 various specialists I was finally diagnosed. There was a cyst on one of my thoracic vertebra that was putting pressure on the nerve that wrapped around my waist. It was keeping me in excruciating and immobilizing pain with the slightest physical movement. I had no life during the entire pain-filled period and I felt doomed. The neurosurgeon that was to do a rare and delicate spinal surgery to remove the cyst was gone for 3 weeks and upon his return I was committed to go under the knife.

It was while waiting for the neurosurgeon to return that a casual friend phoned. She was in the process of writing a book about healers from all over the world and my husband asked her if there was anyone that had something unusually special that might help me. "Oh, yes!" she said, "His name is Max and he's in L.A."

My day nurse rolled me into Max's office in my wheel chair with my husband at my side. Getting out of bed had become such an ordeal for me that I was not the most agreeable person when I met Max and Jennifer. Jennifer was filled with compassion, patience and kindness. Max had an abundance of confidence with an endearing mixture of street toughness and a caring heart.

Max found the negative frequencies that were interfering with my well being and gave me energetic solutions to remove those negative frequencies, then sent me rolling home, saying that they would take about a week to work. For four days, I took the energetic solutions with no change at all. On the fifth morning I opened my eyes after a restless and painful night and discovered that I was completely pain free. Not a twinge. My world had shifted in one sunlit morning. I called Max and he said it was a coincidence.

That was how energetic balancing became part of my life experience. Since that day, any time I am out of balance I either personally see Max or he "zaps" me through my photograph. Energetic balancing has always felt logical and natural to me and has greatly impacted my life and the lives of everyone I have given Max's number. To those who have an open mind, the information in this book will expand the possibilities, opportunities and consciousness of self exploration and discovery.

Lani Hall (Mrs. Herb Alpert)

I have been fortunate enough to have worked with the real Max for over 3 years. I don't know what I would do without him. I am a true believer in his energetic work.

Sanctuary has nothing to do with personal faith — just well being. I don't believe anyone can afford not to be a part of it.

Courteney Cox, actress

Sanctuary reads like a who-done-it. It is exciting and a page turner. Many energetic ideas are studied in some detail to give answers that can indeed work for a vast majority of beings on the planet. Like most ideas and events on the planet, they work "better" if you use them.

Humanity is coming into a newer dimension and expressing itself in a more spiritual/subtle form. Sanctuary is on the cutting edge of many aspects of this emergence. Don't miss out on your own life!

JR (John-Roger Hinkins)
founder of the Church of the
Movement of Spiritual Inner Awareness,
best-selling author of The Spiritual Warrior

I've seen Max do some amazing things, with me and with others. It would be unfortunate for anyone not to avail themselves of energetic balancing.

Burt Bacharach, composer, performer.

A few years ago my wife, Lani, was 3 weeks away from a scheduled major operation to remove a cyst that was leaning on a nerve coming from her thoracic vertebrae (area T-9). The slightest movement would put her in horrific pain. On a flyer and on the recommendation of a friend, we went to see Max with little expectations.

I rolled her into Max's office in a wheel chair and presented Max with her "THUMB." I had never seen anything like that before so I was skeptical at first, but five days after energetic balancing my wife was miraculously pain free and began to resume her normal life. We canceled the operation and on occasion I have seen Max with sometimes astonishing results. The future is here. Check it out.

Herb Alpert, musician, artist

There are few times in our lives when we experience a breakthrough into true consciousness, a deeper awareness of harmony and well-being and the realization that there is so much to the Universe that we haven't even touched upon. Such is the experience of reading "Sanctuary" and its description of our bodies as temple of the living God. I have been blessed to know the real Max Stevens. Through the resources of his ideas, ideals and his miracles, my sense of connectedness has been regenerated and renewed. I encourage everyone to read, savor and deepen from the experience of each section of this book. It is truly an experience that will enrich the body, mind and spirit of all of us.

Tova Borgnine
Chair and CEO, The Tova Corporation

It is an extraordinary gift to be anywhere in the world and be able to make a call about an energetic imbalance and to wake up the next morning feeling great and ready for a new day. We feel everyone should have the opportunity provided by "Sanctuary."

Jerry Moss, co-founder A&M Records
Ani Moss, president of The Dolphin Connection

Sanctuary

The Path to Consciousness

Stephen Lewis
&
Evan Slawson

HTTPress

Published by:
HTTPress, LLC
626 Santa Monica Boulevard, Suite 461
Santa Monica, CA 90401-2538
http://www.httpress.com

To order more copies of this book call toll-free:
877-999-HTTP

ISBN 0-96644334-9

Book's website address: http://www.pathtoconsciousness.com

Printed in the United States of America on acid-free paper

10 9 8 7 6 5 4 3 2 1

FIRST EDITION

Any technology which is sufficiently advanced is indistinguishable from magic.

Robert Heinlein

To know that what is impenetrable to us really exists, manifesting itself as the highest wisdom and most radiant beauty which our dull faculties can comprehend only in their most primitive forms — this knowledge, this feeling, is at the center of true religiousness. In this sense, and in this sense only, I belong to the ranks of devoutly religious men.

Albert Einstein

Take a look round, then, and see that none of the uninitiated are listening. Now by the uninitiated I mean the people who believe in nothing but what they can grasp in their hands, and who will not allow that action or generation or anything invisible can have real existence.

Plato

Those who are not shocked when they first come across quantum theory cannot possibly have understood it.

Niels Bohr

If the doors of perception were cleansed everything would appear to man as it is, infinite.

William Blake

Man's main task in life is to give birth to himself.

Erich Fromm

The present now will later be past.
The order is rapidly fading.

Bob Dylan

Those who are meant to hear will understand.
Those who are not meant to understand will not hear.

Confucius

Contents

Prologue

WHAT IF one day you woke up and realized the world was different than you thought — vastly different? What if you found yourself in the middle of a scientific and spiritual revolution that challenged the very foundations of everything you know about the world around you? What if your sense of certainty about your separateness in the universe could be shattered by the direct experience of oneness with all things? What if that scientific revolution was really a revolution in human consciousness?

How would you feel if the things in your life that block you, slow you down, stop you from being what you've always wanted to be could be vanished? What if your awareness of your connectedness to all things became an earth-shakingly positive experience of the flow of energy in the universe through your mind, body and spirit? If the path to consciousness could be traveled in an instant, would you be ready? Could you step through the looking-glass to see the world as it really is if it meant throwing away your old ideas?

This book is about how I experienced beyond a shadow of a doubt that the world is the way the mystics have said it is. It tells the story of a journey I took. It was a literal and a metaphorical journey in which, step by inexorable step, I came to a place where the truth about the way things really are could no longer be denied. In this place, the energy of the universe surged through me and moved me like a breaker at the beach moves a surfer on a board. You can fight it if you want, and sometimes you manage to get through the breakers to the waves beyond, but there's always another big one coming, and sooner or later it'll get you.

This is the one that got me.

Jane

IN JANUARY of 1996, the size of Jane's universe was precisely defined. It was exactly 4.5 centimeters and located in her uterus. Her greatest fear was that her universe would expand as was already suspected. Apparently, it was expanding into her breasts, her lungs, her brain and her bone marrow. She took no comfort in the fact that the more it expanded the less she would weigh, like some kind of blimp. By now, this 4.5-centimeter asymmetrical tumor was her entire universe: physical, mental, emotional and spiritual. She had no capacity for pleasure. All she had left was this single dark center of consciousness.

In the cold light emanating from the center of that universe, love was out of the question. Even sex... If her universe demanded motion, she went from doctors to gurus to faith healers to charlatans. Now she was on her way back to her doctor. Six weeks of chemotherapy had left her pale, drained and hairless. She felt shaky, weak and alone as she pulled her car into the parking lot at the Pasadena Cancer Clinic.

The glass doors slid apart, admitting Jane from the warm afternoon into the fluorescent overdesigned sterility that felt something like that cold light inside her. Odd how pale the receptionist seemed, looking up and reflecting a wan smile as she recognized Jane from many previous visits. Automatically, numbly, Jane took her usual position in a corner chair, near the magazines, with their hopeful pictures of perfect houses, futures that might be hers, if only they could fit into that tiny universe inside her.

"Doctor will see you now." Another familiar face, a nurse, Jane couldn't think of her name as she dutifully followed into the catacomb of examining rooms. But they turned as soon as they entered, and instead of an examining room, Jane found herself in the doctor's office, staring at a brown desk with a few clinical forms scattered on the glass surface. The wall behind the desk was plastered with degrees, licenses and certifications from the most respected institutions and authorities, as if to reassure that she was in the best of hands, that the care she was receiving was the finest possible within the scope of human knowledge, even of human possibility. The nurse closed the door behind her and Jane waited out the "now" she was promised. That now was an eternity while she carried that universe inside her, but how could these people, these health professionals know. Their job, Jane knew, was to grease the gears in a machine that was bigger than any of them. Her unvoiced fear was that it was a machine that was out of control, that would run over them — run over *her* — at any moment.

The door opened again and Dr. Walker walked in behind her, crossed to his chair and sat down composing his face. Bad news. Jane knew it immediately. She'd seen it enough times. His mouth started moving but no sound came out. There was a ringing in Jane's ears, like the roar of a train or a waterfall, maybe the amplified rush of blood through the capillaries in her eardrums. Maybe it was her own voice screaming.

"...we'll just try it again," he smiled. Did he really smile? Jane's head cleared a little as he waited for her response. She said nothing and the pause made Dr. Walker uncomfortable. "Third time's the trick." No it isn't, his eyes seemed to say. Or maybe Jane's heart was saying it: No more tricks. There were so many questions she wanted to ask, like wasn't the first time supposed to work? Wasn't the second time going to kill that festering growth inside her? Wasn't she too young for this? Wasn't she supposed to have hair? Wasn't she supposed to be having children or playing tennis instead of spending months in these damned clinics, waiting for her chance to drink poison?

"...as you know, for this type of cancer, chemotherapy is the most effective treatment, though some limited success has been reported with radiation treatment and some surgeries have also provided beneficial results." Another pause. Limited success? That would be a relief compared to the ever-expanding universe in her uterus.

"I can't." Her voice seemed to be coming from far away. "I can't do it anymore." Her eyes were downcast and she felt small and helpless.

Dr. Walker looked somber. "This is hard, I know, but it's our only hope." He opened her file. "X-rays don't lie." He slid a series of black-and-white transparencies across the desk. "See for yourself."

She'd seen it before. Her universe, frozen in time, depicted as a glowing ball hovering in her lower abdomen. With all the chemo, all the nausea, all the weakness, all the hair-loss, only the tumor had seemed to prosper, getting ever larger with every dose. Why hadn't he told her that the success rate of such treatment was minuscule? Of course he had trotted out the usual disclaimers, but as if they were an afterthought instead of harsh facts of life.

Seeing her hesitation, Dr. Walker's face darkened. "Look, Jane, let's stop this nonsense. This is your *life* we're talking about. When you fall off the horse, you get right back on and keep on riding. You're not a child anymore. Some choices in life are difficult but you have to make them anyway."

Raising her eyes, Jane was shocked to see the doctor glowering at her, barely restraining his impatience. For a brief moment, he seemed like he filled half the room like a dark cloud. *He won't be satisfied until I'm dead,* was the thought that rolled through her mind in that instant.

"Do the words *very sick* mean anything to you?" he asked. "You're dying."

Jane felt like she was floating in the air above her chair, then, as an afterthought, realized she had stood up. Now she floated to the door.

"Jane? Are you okay? Where are you going?" The doctor's voice came through the roar again.

She saw his name on that fancy gilded degree on the wall behind him. "I'm going home, George," she said, using his first name for a change. After all, what was the point of calling him "doctor?" What good did it do?

He was speechless for a moment, then called "Talk to Ruth up front to schedule an appointment to start the next series." Then his voice was gone like he'd already forgotten her.

Jane knew she wouldn't do it. Enough was enough. This wasn't going to work. She *was* dying. But she couldn't tell what was killing her. Every time she drank the poison she could feel herself dying inside. Even the lab reports confirmed the gradual shut down of her liver. George had said it was normal. Normal to be dying of liver failure by prescription as if the cancer wasn't bad enough. Tears poured down her face as she sped past Ruth, the receptionist, and stalled for a second at the electric doors which seemed to take forever to free her from this glass and steel prison.

The black facade of the medical building loomed behind her like a tombstone over the grave of the parking lot as she fumbled with her keys, climbed into the Mercedes she'd bought a few months earlier. She'd bitterly and ironically thought of it as a going-away present to herself.

She drove hard, the road disappearing under the car, the tears disappearing under the long neck of her sweater. The car seemed to have its own mind and took her on an aimless chase across Los Angeles, until she found herself winding through the high altitude curves of Mulholland Drive, looking out at the city below. Her mind raced faster than the car, thinking back on everything she had been through, the big vistas along the road encouraging big inner vistas, instant replays of the fragments of time and space that led her to this point.

Suddenly she knew where she was going. She took control again, steering the car down into the city, down streets she had known for most of her life, turning again, finally pulling up in front of the massive double doors of a church. She knew this place, hadn't been here in years. But she felt called to be here now. The doors swung on their well-oiled hinges as she slipped into the cool sanctuary of darkness inside. The tall stained-glass windows filled the room with a muted glow. Past the pews, at the far end of the long nave, a shaft of light washed the altar and the crucifix which towered above it. Jane moved into the light and knelt before Christ in his agony and maybe for the first time had some idea what he felt like. And she found her heart talking to God, asking him for comfort, an answer, hope. For that moment, it was as if that universe inside her had vanished, forgotten in the light that flowed around her. She closed her eyes.

"God brings us hope and comfort, though sometimes the answers to our questions are hard to understand." The voice was right beside her. She turned, shocked to recognize the man to whom it belonged. Father Petrov, an old Russian who had long presided over this parish, looked much older than she remembered. He moved in closer, squinting to see her better.

"I know you," he said.

She bowed her head.

He reached out to her. "You have returned in your hour of need."

Jane didn't know what to say. His comments were on target, like direct answers to her prayers of desperation. More memories flooded back to her, attending this church throughout high school, coming back again to get married right after college. She and her husband had attended every week for years, fueled more by his fervor than hers. But when things fell apart between them, he had stayed and she had left to be free of the sense of him and his things which had threatened to suffocate her. Divorce, though it had been stressful, came like a breath of fresh air and she hadn't missed the conformity imposed by this conservative congregation. Now, though, it seemed this church and the kindly old priest were the only place she could find hope.

When Father Petrov asked what brought her here, the tears flowed again and she poured out her story in great sobs. All the while, he stood there, alongside the crucifix, one hand resting lightly on her shoulder, framed by one of the windows, his face without expression as he listened intently. She told him about that universe she carried inside her, the universe that was killing her, the universe that was conspiring with her doctor to kill her. She told him how she had been through chemo twice and how the doctor wanted her to do it again and how she just couldn't and how her car had dragged her here to talk to God. And when she was done talking, there was silence and Father Petrov took both her hands and held them between his own.

He nodded his head and said, "Let us pray."

Together, they sat as he murmured in Latin, in the old way. Without knowing the meaning of the words, Jane felt a sense of comfort, like an awareness of a light within, a blessing received. She looked at him with gratitude, appreciating, if nothing else, the fact that he obviously cared. She felt a meaningful connection with him and, hopefully, through him to God. Father Petrov's prayer ground to a halt. He looked up at her and smiled, sensing that he had succeeded in comforting her. Then Jane blinked or the light shifted and she was forced to look at something she did not want to see. Hopelessness. Something slipped inside her. The magic was gone. But she kept looking anyway. Father Petrov sensed the change immediately, became uncomfortable under her gaze. He cleared his throat.

"You know," he said, "I remember praying here with your mother long ago, just like this, for the exact same reason."

"Do you remember what happened to my mother?" Jane asked, regretting the hint of bitterness in her voice.

"I like to believe her faith gave her some comfort." He paused.

Jane looked at him. "Do you know a prayer that works better than the one you've been using?"

"No, I don't," he said, "but *you* might."

"I don't know anything," Jane said.

"Then you'll have to let God show you the way," Father Petrov finished.

She smiled and touched the priest's hand. Leaving him at the altar, she walked back the way she had come in.

The door swung open and let her out. Without looking back, she climbed into the Mercedes and drove away.

Jane and Terry

JANE CAME HOME to find her house as empty as she left it centuries ago, before the office visit. She sat for a while in her kitchen, listening to the refrigerator run, wondering how much time she had left to be so pleasantly annoyed by the little things in life. And she was crying again when the phone rang. Still crying when the answering machine picked up. Another of several calls from friends asking how she was. She was already dead, so why answer the phone, why return calls from people who were still alive. You can't talk to the dead and they can't talk to you. Or so Jane thought in the depths of her despair at this fork in the road, with her doctor's death sentence waiting around one bend and God's waiting around the other. She hit the erase button, caught her face in the mirror. She pulled off her wig and stared at her bald head in the mirror and suddenly couldn't tell if she was laughing or crying, she was just delirious. Then a confusing sound mixed in with the noise in her head and she finally realized it was the doorbell and what the hell why answer that either.

The doorbell kept at it insistently and someone was calling her name.

"Dammit, Jane, your car's here, I know you're in there. You haven't answered the phone in a week. If you don't open the door, I'll call the fire department to break it down."

The voice of Terry Fisher. Terry had been calling her night and day for months, coming to visit, bringing her food, treating her like an invalid, for God sakes. She was Jane's angel of mercy. Out of all the people who showed they cared, Terry was the one who was always there for her. Her only flaw was maybe a little too much attention, but Jane didn't want to do the proverbial oral examination on her gift horse. She was grateful, but with a slight pique over this untimely interruption of her well-deserved self-pity party. The thought of it ended up in a smile on Jane's face as she hastily pulled her wig back on and opened the door.

Terry, her face fraught with worry, saw the smile. "Hey, what's so funny? I'm worried sick about you, you haven't returned my calls, I'm standing out here for fifteen minutes and you're laughing when you open the door." She hesitated. "Good news?"

Jane's smile faded. So did Terry's.

They stood there without saying another word. They didn't need to speak. Terry knew the drill. She put her arms around Jane and let her put her head on her shoulders. Jane's tears flowed for the millionth time, tattooing mascara onto Terry's blouse.

Then Jane steeled herself and choked back the tears. "I'm done, Terry. I'm done crying. I'm done with doctors. I'm just... Well," Jane dropped her voice. "I'm just done."

Terry squeezed her hard, then held her at arm's length. "You haven't even started yet." They locked eyes and Jane started to quiver. Terry shook her head. "I meant you haven't started to fight for your life. There are still answers, easy answers for this."

Jane went quiet, pulled away. "I'm sorry. Your blouse is ruined."

Something in her tone and the unimportance of the blouse in the scheme of things started Terry laughing. Soon Jane was laughing too.

My House

WHEN I OPENED the door, I was expecting them. Terry's phone call said it was urgent and she was coming over with a friend. So I interrupted my well-deserved rendezvous with a reposado tequila and spent the next twenty minutes doing the dishes and throwing my scattered dirty laundry into a pile next to the washing machine. I may be a slob, but I prefer to keep it to myself. I knew Jane peripherally, found her a little annoying. Terry I knew quite well, found her extremely annoying. We had worked together many times. About the same number of times I tried responding to her flirtations which was in turn the same number of times she rejected me. We were friends. Much to my disappointment.

Terry breezed through the door and gave me a peck on the cheek.

"Hi. You remember Jane, don't you?"

I was stunned. Her sickly-looking companion was nothing like the attractive, curvaceous life-of-the-party I remembered. Her cheeks were hollow and her eyes had no luster, her lips seemed thin and pale. Her clothes hung like they were on a wire hanger.

"You tried to seduce me once," Jane said.

I attempted a smile.

"I told you I was in a relationship then," she said. "But I'm available now."

I stuttered trying to think of something even remotely appropriate. Utterly failing to come up with anything, I motioned for them to come in, gently grabbing Jane's arm to help her inside.

After settling Jane on the couch, I turned to find Terry in my face.

"I've been asking you for help with a friend and you keep turning me down," Terry fumed. "Now," she pointed to Jane, "turn *her* down."

"It's great to see you," I said, dodging the maneuver. "Want some tea?"

Terry followed me into the kitchen where I made a show about finding the tea bags and the kettle and making small talk to continue my evasion.

By the time the water boiled, Jane was fast asleep. I pulled a blanket off my bed and covered her while Terry did her thing with the tea bags. As I covered Jane up, she curled into a fetal position and sighed softly. Her face was drawn. I felt a pang of sorrow as I stood over her. I turned as Terry pushed a steaming mug in front of me. I took it gratefully. Terry's eyes told me she understood what I was feeling. She tilted her head towards the kitchen and we tiptoed out of the room.

Sitting in the stylish glare of a halogen lamp dangling over the table, Terry filled me in on Jane's day up until they arrived at my door. I listened quietly.

"You're her only hope," Terry finished.

"Me? I'm a commercial director. Currently unemployed."

"Between jobs," Terry insisted.

I tried to smile. "Terry, she has terminal cancer. What am I supposed to do for her? Yell 'Cut?'"

An unmistakably homicidal look slid across her face.

"Just kidding," I put my hands up in mock surrender.

"I want you to bring her to Max," Terry said.

"I can't," I said.

"You can and you will," Terry said. "Or you'll go in there and tell her you won't."

"Max isn't around," I said.

Terry held my gaze. "You know where he is." It was a simple statement, one that was more or less true.

Max Stevens. A close friend who disappeared, which is partly why Terry came to me to find him. The other part is the reason she was trying to find him at all: the fact that Max knew things about healing, though he never called it that. He talked about energy and life force and spirit. But ultimately, when he was done with you, you felt better than you ever had before. Though he steadfastly refused to claim that he could *cure* anything, I had seen his clients come in the door with every imaginable ailment and within weeks, usually days, sometimes hours, report that all of their symptoms were gone. Symptoms that they'd had for years, sometimes their whole lives. My own father had come in with diagnosed prostate cancer. The day his test results came back, his doctors insisted he needed immediate surgery. I insisted that he go see Max instead. After some vehement arm-twisting, he capitulated. For six whole weeks, he took the drops Max gave him, putting them under his tongue as instructed. The entire time, he complained that he didn't believe in this and it wasn't going to work. At Max's request he submitted to being checked again after three weeks. Max adjusted the drops he was taking. At the end of six weeks, he returned for a third visit and Max told him that he couldn't find any trace of the things he came in with. A few days after that he went to the doctor again, asking for the prostate test to be repeated. The new test showed that he was cancer free. His doctors claimed they must have made a mistake the first time.

"He's not doing it anymore," I told her. "He's developing something new and doesn't want to be interrupted. And I promised to respect his wishes."

Terry threw a quick glance through the door at Jane on the couch.

"She's going to die." Terry set her jaw and looked at me like it was my fault.

The fact was that Jane had been directed to Max years ago, after her cancer was first diagnosed. She had called him up and told him that she wanted him to cure her.

"I don't cure cancer," Max had said, as he always did.

Jane had insisted that people told her he cured diseases. Any disease, including cancer, AIDS and the common cold.

"I don't cure anything," he repeated. "I detect disturbances in the subtle energy fields which control all your life
processes, physical, mental, emotional and spiritual. Then I
bring those disturbances back into balance."

"That's it?" she had asked.

"That's it," Max replied.

"What about curing diseases?"

"Cures imply medical diagnostic techniques and corol-
laries to those techniques. That's not what I do."

So Jane thanked him for his time, saying that this didn't
sound like anything she needed right now, then hung up the
phone, despite the protests of her friends like Terry who
had been using these energetic balancing regimens for years
and had experienced a great sense of well-being and freedom from illness as a result. The story mirrored so many
others. There were people who preferred tragedy and
complexity to winning the easy way, it seemed. Jane was
one of them. I almost wanted to laugh when I first heard
her reaction, but inside I knew it was a death sentence for
her. Terry had twisted my arm to talk to her and I tried.
But everything I said was greeted with an uninformed,
willfully ignorant skepticism. I tried introducing her to the
underlying concepts as I understood them. Much of the
material I showed her was accompanied by an extensive,
well-tested literature, but she rejected it based on the fact
that her MD knew nothing about it. Finally I gave up, despite Terry's protests.

"You can't give up," she pushed.

"Terry, who is this woman to judge Max's work?" I asked her. "She skipped high school physics but thinks she's qualified to dismiss the entire field of quantum mechanics. And she thinks we're fools who've been suckered into believing in a fraud."

Now Jane was back. After chasing down the best doctors and the most lethal "cures," she wanted to try again what she had rejected. Unfortunately, it might not be that easy. Max had shut down his office and, like the guy in the old television show Green Acres, bought some land in the middle of nowhere. He was now doing who knows what, who knows where. In addition, he would probably remember her and might refuse to have anything to do with her since she had already come to him, then changed her mind. He had long maintained a policy which fully supported those who didn't feel his techniques were for them. Generally speaking, this included encouraging them not to come back, if not insisting that they stay as far away as possible. "Why waste time convincing people," he said, "when there are so many people who already want to do this work?"

"We'll take that chance," Terry said. She handed me the phone. "Call him."

"I don't know if he has a phone and if he does I don't have the number."

"Then where is he? We'll go there." She looked into my eyes, searching. "And don't tell me you don't know, either. You always know where he is."

That's what irritated me about her the most. She usually knew what I was thinking, sometimes before I did. Max had always said she had a strong intuition, which I felt pretty sure was a synonym for being a pain in the ass.

"I *don't* know," I said. And I didn't. "Not exactly."

"Then go in there," she indicated the living room, "and tell Jane *something*... and I want to hear what you say."

The Road

AN HOUR LATER we were heading east out of Los Angeles in my Jeep. Terry had wanted us to drive her Volvo, but based on the vague directions Max had left me, I thought we needed something that would go anywhere. Jane was sleeping fitfully in the back seat and Terry was staring out into the night. That left me alone with the road, the car and the thoughts in my head.

I hadn't seen Max in months. He left for the wilderness like some modern John the Baptist. Unlike John the Baptist, he had not yet returned and he also left a standing invitation to join him at any time. A full schedule of being a shill for dancing toilet paper and singing mayonnaise had prevented my embarking on that particular adventure, though I had managed to cultivate a sunburn in Mexico on one otherwise forgettable weekend away from the grind. Now, things in the gee-whiz biz were suffering, or maybe I was suffering, so I had backed off from the greater cause of building media careers for assorted consumer goods in order to scale the mountain of self-doubt and ennui. Jane's crisis was a first-class excuse for me to attempt my acrobat-

ics of consciousness in some quiet corner of the great out-
doors. Max's preliminary descriptions of the rustic accom-
modations on his newly purchased hideaway left me vaguely
hoping he had at least fixed the roof.

As the low rumble of the Jeep's V-8 floated us far into
the great western desert, I thought about how far things
had come to be headed this way at all. My friend Max had
been a successful doctor with a large and still-growing practice when his interests in various healing practices led him
into other areas. Over time, he covered many disciplines in
great depth. These disciplines included acupuncture, bio-
feedback, oriental medicine, ayurveda and homeopathy.
Gradually, these interests eclipsed his more conventional
training.

Little by little he incorporated previously-existing methodologies and systems and then developed his own methods
of analysis. He began measuring what he called "subtle energies." These energies, though incredibly tiny and difficult
to measure, combine in the infinite multiplicity of the universe to become the greatest and most powerful energies,
ranging from the nuclear holocaust that we call the sun, to
the breath of life in our bodies. Each thing that existed
could be identified by its unique energetic "fingerprint," if
only one knew how to read it. Max had figured this out to
an unprecedented level of detail. Using his knowledge of
physics and electronics he began delving into the application
of computers to this new area.

His system made it possible to do phenomenally complex energetic analysis very rapidly. Most remarkable, ex-

panding on techniques which had been used by homeopaths for over a hundred years, he developed the ability to use frequencies to identify and neutralize the unique energetic signatures associated with many maladies. Well, that's not strictly true... The strict truth is that he'd developed the ability to use subtle energy frequencies to identify and neutralize the energetic signatures associated with virtually *all* maladies. Though, as he constantly emphasized, it was not considered scientifically correct to presume that the frequency and the physical disease were the same thing.

I had met Max through a mutual friend. Through Terry actually. At that time, I was a run-down mess. I was physically and emotionally burned out from long shooting schedules, doing work that often wasn't aligned with what I really wanted to do. Yoga, which I had practiced for years, fell out of my life because I was simply too tired. Then my digestion went awry. Food didn't agree with me. My skin suddenly changed from smooth and elastic to scaly, dry and itchy. I had never had allergies to anything, but it seemed like I was becoming allergic to everything. I constantly had a sore throat. My back hurt. I felt lousy all the time. I didn't know where to turn, either.

I had given up on MD's nearly twenty years earlier. Sometime in my early sex life, I had contracted a venereal disease which manifested a small amount of pus for a few days, along with painful urination. No, it wasn't gonorrhea. Too obvious. So for a year, I underwent culture tests and blood tests and took antibiotics and shots of gamma globulin. The results were always the same: no change.

The diagnosis was always the same, too: "non-specific urethritis." This meant they agreed I actually had a disease, but they had no idea what it was. Though the painful urination went away, the disease didn't.

A period of employment as night librarian at a medical school gave me an opportunity to pore through textbooks and course materials as well as watch instructional videos on techniques and procedures. Slowly it dawned on me just how much doctors had to know in order to know nothing at all. Their detailed explanations of metabolism and body function and neural function, etc., were at best merely *descriptions* of biological processes. These descriptions substituted detail for understanding. Comparing the dogmatic authority doctors wield in our lives with the information I had at my fingertips, I finally realized the pointlessness and uselessness — and sometimes *dangerousness* — of the advice and potions they dispensed. Even their primary weapon, antibiotics, had lost its power, a fact that epidemiologists freely acknowledged. I found myself further discouraged by their willingness to march blindly and obediently in lockstep with the party line: Though most people weren't aware of it, MDs weren't allowed to make their own judgement about handling their cases. Instead, they were forced by state, federal and insurance company regulations to hew a narrow course of prescribed solutions to almost every condition. In addition, they were unwittingly perpetrating a sinister conspiracy, that their dogma was the only truth. Their work as healers was over and their work as minions of a technocracy had begun. Despite their assurances, platitudes and prescriptions, my symptoms persisted. Inevitably, in the absence of being run over by a truck, I gave up on MDs for good.

So I suffered with my ailments and sadly chalked it up to the aging process. But I knew it was something else, something more concrete. I just didn't know who might be able to identify it or deal with it. That was where Terry came in. I had met Terry when she played a very nice-looking can of tuna in a national spot that I was directing. We became friends. One day, over drinks, she told me about Max, a doctor she was going to who could deal with allergies effectively.

"So he's some kind of allergist?" I said. "I've been to them."

"Not exactly," she replied. "He actually deals with anything. That's his specialty. For example, I used to have herpes and now I don't."

"He cured you of herpes?" I asked, cynically.

"He says he didn't," Terry told me. "But all I know is I don't have outbreaks anymore and I don't take drugs for it."

"How does he explain that?"

"He says the frequency of herpes is gone and if I want the disease diagnosed or treated, I should go to a doctor." She shrugged, coyly, and took a sip from her mai-tai. "But why bother since I never have outbreaks. I'm sure you're glad to hear that."

I was. "Did he take you off your drugs?"

"No," she said, "he'll never do that. He says it's between me and my doctor. But I just didn't think I needed
them anymore and I guess I was right."

I'd heard enough. "I want to see this guy."

"And I want you to see him," she said, "if you're going
to be seeing me."

She gave me the phone number and said she would
provide the necessary referral, because he accepted new
business only via direct personal referral by existing clients.

I called immediately and was told that there were no ap-
pointments available until October. It was February. I
booked it anyway. It might be great, I reasoned, if I lasted
until October. In the meantime, I got worse. Every month
or so I called to see if somebody had canceled, hoping an
earlier appointment might open up. On a particularly bad
day when my face was swollen and my throat was sore and
I felt like I'd been sleeping in a poison ivy patch, I called
again. Still nothing. But luck was on my side. Half an
hour later, Max's office called back to tell me that someone
had canceled an appointment for the next day.

I showed up at the office in a small building in Santa
Monica. For a change I was on time. I had been warned
that being late was unacceptable and missing my appointment meant I would never be seen again. The attitude in
his office was that those transgressions endangered others
who might have used the time to improve their own well-
being.

"People sometimes die before they get their chance to go
to him," Terry had confided.

When I was led into his office, it was nothing like I expected, though I had no idea *what* to expect. It was pleasant and simple and I was offered a chair on the opposite side of Max's desk. Max was nothing like I expected either, though my expectations of him exactly matched my expectations of his office. He was powerfully built, in his fifties, with short dark hair and a steady gaze.

"Let's see your thumb," he said.

Confused, I hesitated.

"That's the finger closest to your shoulder," he said pleasantly.

"I know which one it is," I said irritably, sticking it out.

"Just trying to be helpful." He looked at my thumb. "Great. Now open your other hand."

I did and he dropped a shiny metal cylinder into it. The metal cylinder had a wire attached to it. He hit a few buttons on a keyboard and the computer monitor on his desk filled with a grid full of cryptic abbreviations. He grabbed my thumb, picked up a pointing device with a brass tip attached to another wire and pressed the thing against a spot on the side of the thumb. The computer made an electronic whooping noise. I stared at the monitor, trying to comprehend what he was doing.

"What does that mean?" I asked.

"It means you're still alive." he replied.

For the next forty-five minutes, Max tapped keys on the keyboard, pressed the pointing device against my thumb and listened to the whooping noise. It was accompanied by a visual reference, a kind of meter on the side of the screen.

Screenful after screenful of the abbreviations flitted by and he made comments occasionally as he worked.

"What is your dominant weakness?" he asked.

"I don't know," I replied.

"I wasn't asking you." Max grinned. "I was telling you what question I was asking the machine."

A few screens later he said, "You have back pain, right?"

Definitely not, I told him.

"Sure you do. Up between your shoulder blades."

I insisted that my back was fine. I was thinking about my lower back, which I gratefully had always been on good terms with.

"No, no. Up higher, between the shoulder blades," he repeated.

Suddenly it clicked. "You mean thoracic pain," I agreed.

"How am I supposed to know if you know a thoracic vertebrae from the exit to your gastrointestinal system," he laughed.

I explained that I thought he was talking about lumbar pain. Then I told him that for years I'd had regular chiropractic adjustments for a thoracic vertebra that refused to stay adjusted.

"It's hard to adjust and the pain comes back in about an hour," he offered.

I was amazed. How did he know?

"You have a frequency imbalance which usually manifests itself like that," he said. "It'll be gone in a few days."

Well, okay. What could I say? I thought I was going to some kind of allergy specialist. I had no idea what I was in for. I tried to follow the screens as he flipped through each one, applying the pointer to my thumb. It was nearly impossible. Too much information on each screen made for quick overload. Meanwhile, Max kept telling me about myself.

"You have the frequency of cancer on..." Max paused as he flipped to another screen. "Your mother's side." He put the pointer down. "Is there cancer in your mother's family?"

My mother had been battling cancer for ten years, I acknowledged.

"You understand that the things I am finding don't constitute a clinical diagnosis of disease." Max studied my reaction as I waited for him to continue. "What I do is find energetic imbalances, subtle energy frequencies which have traditionally been associated with disease, but are not in themselves evidence of disease." He waited again.

I didn't understand, if understanding meant some profoundly deep grasping of the ideas he was presenting, but I had done yoga for many years and had experienced both subtle and not-so-subtle manifestations of the movement of inner energies which are largely unexplained outside of the yogic disciplines. I nodded and he expounded further.

"Your body is telling me that you have the energetic potential for cancer. This energetic potential is hereditary and you got it from your mother's side of your family. It can and will be removed. As a result, it will be difficult for your body to support the energy specific to manifesting an active physical cancer. In classical homeopathy, this energetic potential for disease has been recognized for more than a century. Homeopaths call hereditary energetic potentials *miasms*. The frequency which indicated your back pain is different. It isn't a miasm. It's an energetic imbalance which, energetically speaking, has become active. By application of the correct balancing frequency to counter the active imbalance, the imbalance disappears." Max paused. "Technically, of course, since I don't diagnose or treat disease, if your back pain goes away, you should consider it a coincidence."

I looked at him, questioning.

Max shrugged. "Just trying to be helpful. Seems most people view life as an unwieldy clump of coincidences. And the others are probably just paranoid."

Back to the machine. More of my long-time complaints were identified by Max. He looked up. "You have the frequency of an infection in the frequency of your urethra."

For a moment, I was dumbfounded, then I remembered the non-specific urethritis. In the midst of all my more current woes, I had forgotten about the venereal disease I had contracted so long ago. I had always known it was there, but after giving up on doctors I had given up on the non-specific urethritis.

"You're finding that in the frequency of my thumb?" I waved my hand.

"No," he said. "That's actually your thumb."

Max pressed a few more buttons, ran through a few more screens. "You've had this a long time. Maybe twenty years."

I told him about the history of my unidentified infection.

"The vibrational imbalance that I've detected will go away within a few days," he said.

"How about the symptoms?" I asked.

"I believe you can look forward to experiencing a coincidence."

After Max was done with me, his tall, blonde girlfriend Jennifer took me into her office, where she produced a series of bottles of clear liquid which had droppers in their lids. She punched up each of the energetic things Max had identified on a similar computer at her desk. One at a time, she placed each bottle on a metal plate which was wired through some electronic boxes to her computer.

"These are your remedies," she said. "The computer is imprinting subtle energy frequencies into the bottles. The energetic imprint lasts about a month. Don't expose the remedies to magnetic fields, like airport metal detectors, because they can erase the imprinted frequencies."

She explained how to take the remedies by first "activating" the energy in them by tapping them against my hand, then putting ten drops under my tongue. I had to do this every half hour for the first day, every two or three hours on the second day, then three times a day for the next four days. Some of the bottles were smaller and were to be taken on a different schedule.

"These are for your hereditary frequencies. Take three drops before bed, but only use one bottle per night."

I was curious why. She told me that some people found it uncomfortable when the miasms were being released. "Many people report that they have very vivid dreams and often they have aches and pains generated by the release of their miasms."

Not knowing what to expect, other than Terry's tireless advocacy of whatever it was Max did, I started what was to become a ritual for the next few weeks. I had to avoid mint before and after taking the drops. I had to avoid food for half an hour before and after and avoid water for fifteen minutes before and after.

As the weeks passed, I found that all the problems I had been experiencing fell away. For the first time in years, I had lots of energy. Emotionally I felt great. The long-time symptoms related to the non-specific urethritis were gone. My reaction to all this was amazement.

A month later, I went back for a follow-up visit. He found a few more things. Everything he found was accompanied by a description of what I should be feeling according to the presence of that particular energetic frequency. He was always right on. Max told me that energetic work was like peeling away the layers of an onion. As each outer layer was removed, it revealed another layer underneath it.

I wanted to know more about what he was doing. Jennifer recommended a book on "vibrational medicine," which I purchased on my way home. As I sat back to take my drops, I started reading. The book described a large body of well-documented historic and recent techniques for energetic diagnosis and for remedying accompanying imbalances, and gave illustrations that were easy to understand and on some level made sense. The techniques described weren't the same thing as what Max was doing to me. But they showed me that there were others who believed in and worked with subtle energy phenomena. Max seemed to have achieved an undreamed-of level of precision with his approach to this work. My reaction to the information in the book was mixed: I knew that if I hadn't already experienced for myself that Max's techniques worked I would think that the book was the biggest load of crap I had ever read. But now, in the face of the reality I had already experienced, it provided information that helped me understand that the incredible work Max was doing was at least *possible*.

In the years before I got into the commercials business, I had worked with computers and had developed an unusual set of skills. As I watched Max work, I was alternately amazed at his accomplishments and appalled at his relatively primitive tools — by my standards, that is. I urged him to allow me to make some changes. At first, Max ignored everything I said. Finally one day, I irritated him enough for him to ask just how I would do it. I suggested a number of procedural changes, to start with. I came back the next day with some floppy disks and installed some software on his computer. He tried it, looked at me and said "You're actually right." It was faster, better, more efficient. That began a new dimension in our relationship. And eventually Max routinely asked my advice about implementing changes. Ultimately, Max became dependent on me to keep up with a technology that changed schizophrenically. And even though I was out of the computer business, I continued to provide my expertise for his particular and very unusual applications. In the process we became close friends.

In the years since I had first met Max, it was as if a plague had begun to take over the world. AIDS had become one of the biggest killers in the country, crossing lines of gender, sexuality and location. Recent murmurings from various official sources began to hint that it was no longer just limited to transmission by bodily fluids like blood and semen. The sinister word was that saliva was a threat as well and that HIV, the rapidly mutating retrovirus reputed to cause AIDS, might have even mutated to become an airborne strain, as was possible with any retrovirus. Tuberculosis was ubiquitous to the point where television news reports warned about contracting the disease on long plane flights. Some news reports called Southern California the tuberculosis capital of the United States, saying the incidence of infection was as high as eighty-five percent of the population due in part to lax inspection practices in Southern California's beef slaughterhouses. According to these reports, carcasses with visible sores could not be disqualified as sellable until a lab report proved the presence of TB. The necessary tests took weeks; in the meantime the carcasses were butchered and sold. Other diseases, like the Hanta virus and Lyme disease and the dreaded African hemorrhagic fevers including Marburg, tacaribe and Ebola were found throughout the United States, although reported only in relatively isolated cases. Headlines blared news about people getting hepatitis from infected strawberries, hemorrhagic *E. coli* from hamburger, mercury toxicity from fish, and aluminum from grated cheese. All over the world, people would read the paper and, in desperation, delete one food after another from their diets. An entire high-priced food industry had arisen by advertising "disease-free, contaminant-free" food. Food processing companies were alternately scrambling to add preservatives to extend the shelf-life of their products, then scrambling to remove them when they proved to be carcinogenic. In California, forests were routinely closed to campers due to epidemics of bubonic plague, a.k.a. yersinia pestis, the scourge of medieval Europe, in the rodent populations.

I remember Max laughing about that.

"If they're going to close the campgrounds, they have to close the Hollywood Hills and the Santa Monica Mountains and the whole of Los Angeles — especially Beverly Hills and Malibu — while they're at it," he said. "They think the fleas and squirrels don't migrate? That they stay in the parks and forests, respecting the boundaries? Maybe they think the rats can read. If so, they should make little signs, in Rode-ish, saying 'Achtung rodents und vermin! Private property! Verboten!'"

The medical system was overwhelmed and, worse, was usually unable to identify or treat the diseases which were traveling throughout the country. Though the doctors in the trenches of the war on disease routinely prescribed antibiotics, they failed to obtain the tests required to accurately identify the infecting organisms. Because antibiotics are relatively specific to each organism, they were rarely matched correctly. Even worse, the improper use of these drugs, both in humans and in the animals grown for meat, had resulted in the once-susceptible organisms becoming vaccinated against the effects of antibiotics. Now, almost laughably, some microorganisms had become dependent on antibiotics and would thrive until the patient stopped taking the antibiotics, at which point the organisms would die without them. Medical researchers in the field of epidemiology had concluded that all antibiotics were now totally ineffective, despite their continued use by medicine men. Nobody I knew felt well anymore. Nobody, that is, except Max's clients. His energetic practice had grown to several thousand people who depended on his energetic balancing techniques to sustain them.

Though Max continued to stress that energetic imbalance was not necessarily correlated to disease, it appeared not to be unrelated. I knew that whenever I felt unwell, a visit to Max and the dutiful taking of drops always resulted in feeling better. The frequencies he detected usually were associated with some disease, though they were not, as Max pointed out, the disease themselves. But if these frequencies were any indication, the prevalence of serious disease was even greater than that recognized by medical authorities. After all, without explicit and specific testing, doctors could only guess at the organisms underlying such vague descriptions as "cold" and "flu."

*   *   *

We were hours out of the city. A stream of signs blurred by, trumpeting the colorful names of the one-horse desert towns which dotted the series of desert basins we were passing through. Their names usually told the story of their origin. Garlock and Ludlow and Amboy were old whistle stops where steam trains had stopped for water long ago, now reduced to ruins sometimes decorated with rusting automobiles and a few mobile homes. Others with names like Lodestone, Leadville, Goldfield, Iron Mountain and Silver City once supported the mining of the rich mineral deposits which made the sparsely vegetated land both so stark and so majestic. South Fork, Deep Valley and Devil's Hole were named for their geography. Names like Caliente and Baker were wry comments on the local weather. As the sun began to wash the sky in the east, we turned off the main highway following the vague directions Max had given me. This turn was the last of the actual instructions. From this point, the directions were some form of riddle. "Get the monkey off your back" was the next clue.

The stiff springs in the Jeep betrayed every bump on the shoulderless two-lane road and Terry soon stirred in the passenger seat beside me. I glanced at her as she stretched herself, then turned to look at Jane, sleeping deeply in the back seat. She turned back to me, her face creased with worry.

"Should I drive faster?" I quipped, trying to cheer her up.

"Just keep your eyes and the car on the road," she said without a trace of humor.

She stared out into the desert, watching it light up in the pinks and golds of dawn. We were in an area of gently rolling land, laced with arroyos and spotted with outcroppings of granite the size of small houses, rounded smooth by millennia of exposure to the harsh desert winds and the floods which sometimes bore down out of the mountains looming up ahead. The road was arrow-straight for more than twenty miles, but now it was starting to twist and curve gently as it headed into the hills. Ahead of us, it snaked into the distance and disappeared.

"This is the middle of nowhere," Terry commented.

"You say that like it's a bad thing," I replied.

"How much farther?"

I glanced at her. "I have a confession to make. I don't have any idea where we're going from here." I tossed her Max's letter. "Check this out."

She scanned the letter. "This is weird. Is he out of his mind?"

"Maybe this is the only way he knows to get there," I teased.

"Maybe he's trying to prevent lesser beings from finding him," she answered. "And he's succeeding, I think."

Ignoring her, I scanned the pre-dawn horizon looking for some solution. The distant ridgelines were going to be our destination, it seemed.

"Look for something shaped like a monkey." I indicated the edge of the sky.

Her eyes followed the highway until it dissolved in the shadowy depths of the desert, then on to the mountains. We drove in silence a bit, then she pointed a slender finger.

"What about that?"

I tried to make out the shape she was indicating. "I don't see it."

"Look at the flat-topped mountain —"

"The mesa..."

"The mesa," she continued. "Then follow it to the left, there's kind of a dome-shaped part. Maybe that's it."

"I don't buy that's a monkey. How about that set of spires over there? Can you picture it as a monkey raising its arms?"

She looked and laughed. "It looks like a collection of sea shells."

"Maybe we just have to drive further." I stepped into the gas pedal so the jeep would eat the miles and quickly spit them out the back.

"We're not lost, are we?" Terry looked concerned.

I tossed her the map and quickly tapped our location as she unfolded it. "We're here."

She studied the map. That gave me an idea.

"Those markings," I showed her, "Those are the topographical shapes of the mountains. Look for a monkey shape in the contours of the mountains as seen from above."

She pored over the swirling lines. "There's nothing here," she concluded.

"It's got to be here," I replied. "Max wouldn't just lead us on some wild goose chase."

"No," she pointed to the map. "Nothing. It's a town. It's near here. There's another one called Empty. Dry. Rhesus. Gorp. These are weird names." She looked closer to read another name.

"Wait!" I shouted. "What did you say?"

"I said these are weird names."

"Before that!"

"The names — Dry, Gorp, Rhesus —"

"That's it." I slammed my hand on the wheel. "Rhesus is a type of monkey." I looked at her. "There's really a town called Rhesus?"

She showed me the map and sure enough, it was there. It lay at the end of a tangled web of back roads leading deep into the high desert mountains."

"Keep your eyes on the road," she cautioned.

"You navigate," I replied.

Rhesus. Jesus. I didn't want to know what it was named for. I was just glad we were on track. The miles howled away behind us. We followed a series of turns and the road began to climb. As we crested the last of the low foothills, a green valley spread out below us, an oasis in the desert. Pleasant rectangles of cultivated crops checkered the bottomlands. On the other side of the valley lay what I presumed was the town of Rhesus. It sprawled part-way up into the hills behind it, gleaming white in the light of morning. From this distance it looked like a hillside village in a mythical land that time forgot, Mykonos or Corfu for instance. I glanced at Terry. She was smiling, more comfortable at the sight of civilization after miles of nothing.

We soon lost our view of it as the road took us down to the valley floor.

Twenty minutes later Terry and I were comfortably ensconced at a table in a sterile chrome and glass cafe that could be mistaken for an operating room, if not for the large view windows overlooking a lush nine-hole desert golf course and the steaming bowls of cappuccino on the table in front of us. Jane was still asleep in the truck; we had elected to let her rest, leaving a note on the dashboard telling her where we were.

To Terry's dismay, Max's new abode was not in town. He had used this place as the jumping off place for a further series of riddles which would lead us to him. Not knowing how long it would be before we found him, I filled the gas tank and suggested fueling our stomachs before continuing the journey. The town turned out to be a conglomerate of modern and Spanish style buildings. None of the restaurants around the town square was open, so we drove around until we stumbled across the golf course and its cafe.

Our fellow diners had an average age of a hundred and seven, judging loosely by the gray hair, wrinkled skin and nightmarish pale plaid, white-shoed outfits they wore in preparation for their tee times. We got a few stares but they soon returned to their lost-ball-in-the-rattlesnake-infested-mesquite stories. The narrow greens dog-legged through rough terrain featuring ocotillo, tall cacti, jagged granite and, one would presume, the occasional rattlesnake. Terry stirred her coffee and I stirred my oatmeal, hoping the cereal would settle the queasy stomach I had developed on the long ride.

"Why did he leave?"

She was asking about Max. I pretended to ignore her, poring over the rough scrawl which held the clues to our destination. A light but well-placed whack on the shin shifted my attention.

"Don't ignore me," she said. "He must have told you."

But I wasn't sure I should tell her. Max had taken me into his confidence and explained a lot of the depth of the energetic work that he was doing.

All along, he insisted that it was something other than medicine. That was a point that was always a bone of contention between us. To me, it was medicine, even though the explanations were more esoteric and used substantially different methodologies. When he said "frequency" I heard "disease." But he steadfastly denied it. These arguments would invariably end with an agreement to disagree.

Little by little, though, I realized Max was taking a path even *I* couldn't understand. At first, I thought he was just plain wrong. The resistance he encountered from the medical community led him further and further into his energetic alternatives. Finally he declared that the western system of medicine was incurably limited by its false beliefs in a universe governed by Newtonian physics. Material realism is what he called it. In principle, I agreed, but urged him not to abandon attempts to get academic recognition of his work, so it could be made available to the endless hordes of the sick.

"You get it and you don't get it," he said. "You abandoned your own beliefs in western medicine long before you met me, then try to tell me you want me to waste my time convincing them that they're all wrong. Why don't you do it yourself?"

I didn't have an answer.

"Your problem," he continued, "is that you're still stuck in paternalism, somehow you still want to please them, you still want agreement from these so-called authority figures. We've been through this over and over. Nothing has changed. You're like a Model-T mechanic trying to fix a supercomputer. Why is it unacceptable for you to have a negative frequency? Why do you have to give it a name like Hansen's Disease? Did Hansen give it to you? If you can't breathe, who cares if it's called a Koch bacillus? I identify frequencies, not micro-organisms. Maybe there are problems which have no frequency associated with them, in which case you need to see an MD, because I deal with frequencies. If you have a problem with no frequency, I can't help you. On the other hand if you have a frequency imbalance I can help you, but I can't tell you whether or not you have a micro-organism because I don't measure those. Maybe you're tired because of a frequency you have, or maybe it's because Mr. Epstein and Mr. Barr attacked you. If it's the latter, you should pay them a visit."

He went on to talk about Heisenberg's uncertainty principle: In the late 1800's, Werner Heisenberg, a German scientist, had developed a mathematical model which showed that we could only know either the position or the momentum of an electron, but never both, because to know one factor destroyed both our capability to know the other factor and the existence of the other factor. Though it described subatomic phenomena, it applied equally well to so-called "real-world" events. For instance, if we know how fast a train is moving, we cannot say with certainty where it is, because it is, in fact, moving. In order to determine the precise position of the train, we must destroy its momentum, its forward speed. At the moment we fix its position, its speed can no longer be known with certainty. As soon as we try to determine its speed again, our certain knowledge of its position evaporates.

"Oddly enough," Max pointed out, "many of my clients have experienced a parallel to this. Medical diagnosis of their condition seems to become more ambiguous as their energetic balance changes." He smiled. "Perhaps we should think of their medical diagnosis as their position and their energetic balance as their momentum."

Over time he went further and further out there in terms of his work with frequencies. He told me about measuring frequencies of more ethereal things, metaphysical things.

"Are they real?" I asked him.

"What does that mean?" he challenged. "Every frequency is real. Your question is 'Is it relevant?'"

"Your work with identifying real physical things using subtle-energy techniques is fine," I said, as if my approval was needed to validate his work. "But now you're identifying frequencies of things which otherwise aren't known to exist. How do we know these things are real?"

Max eyeballed me and I couldn't tell whether he was even taking me seriously or not. Finally, he replied. "You've opened a can of worms if you really want me to address your question. First we have to ask: Is reality an objective fixed thing or is it culturally biased, something created out of consensus? If it's objective, then is our perception of it capable of seeing it objectively? Linguistically, you're in a bind because you might be implying that you can subjectively see something objective and you're caught in a paradox."

As I struggled to come up with a rebuttal, he continued. "Can you perceive the universe? It's bigger than your vision. It's bigger than your concept of it, unless you expand considerably. If you can't contain it, or stand outside of it to see it clearly, you lose all hope of true objectivity. In other words, to answer your question, if it can be detected it has reality."

"What do you mean by 'detected?'" I asked.

"Perceived," he replied.

As I thought about it, he continued: "We've been using the word *see* as a synonym for *perceive*. That's an important point as well. What if you can't see it? What if it has to be perceived in another way? Thousands of years ago, Plato said 'Take a look round, then, and see that none of the uninitiated are listening. By the uninitiated I mean the people who believe in nothing but what they can grasp in their hands, and who will not allow that action or generation or anything invisible can have real existence.' So your dilemma isn't new, is it?"

Still, his new direction didn't sit right with me. "What's wrong with maintaining a focus on a subtle-energy interpretation of the world as we know it?" I asked him.

"The world as we know it is an unncecessary limitation," he explained. "Where would the world be if Columbus had stuck to the world as it was known then, or Galileo, or Newton, or Einstein, or Edison? We're exploring a new frontier. I want to see how far things can go, how far the unknown river will take me."

Finally, his exploration took him to the point where he abandoned the world of orthodox medicine altogether and totally immersed himself in the metaphysical implications of his work. He put his medical license into inactive status and closed his hugely successful medical practice. For a little while, he ran an "energetic consulting" practice which quickly became as well attended as his previous medical business. But he grew impatient with it. "I'm wasting time with the small stuff."

"Small?" I exclaimed, incredulous. "You're curing cancer."

"I cure nothing. I only direct your energy. And if I can do that, why live with the limits of your perceptions?"

"What are your limits?" I asked Max.

"Hopefully, I'll never know," he said. "I can be satisfied with my work, but I'll never be content with it."

We debated further and he asked, "How many times have you told me you feel better than you've ever felt?"

I just looked at him and he continued:

"Does each time you said that include the previous times?"

I acknowledged they did.

"What makes you think that next time won't include this time?" he demanded.

I laughed and said I figured I was perfect.

"This is serious," Max said. "I'm on the verge of a breakthrough. I've found a much more subtle, tenuous and promising path and I need you to walk it with me."

"What are you saying?" I asked.

"I'm not sure yet," he said. "I'm still thinking it through."

I had no idea what he was talking about, but without hesitation knew I had to be part of it.

"So where are we going?" I asked.

"We're not sure," he said. "But we know how to get there."

What I knew was that he had worked miracles on me. I felt better than I ever had, so I had no need to visualize anything else. But Max was convinced that the true value of his work had not yet been realized.

Then suddenly, he disappeared. My phone rang non-stop as his clients that knew me called to ask where he had gone. I was clueless. A few weeks later I got a letter from him containing cryptic directions to his location and an equally cryptic note of triumph claiming dramatic and powerful new discoveries, along with what I can only call a "summary invitation" to see for myself. As it happened, Jane's impending demise hastened my immediate departure.

Terry's voice brought me out of my reminiscence.

I spooned the last of my oatmeal out of the bowl, finished my coffee and said "Let's get out of here."

We walked to the car. As I opened the door for her, she turned before getting in and grabbed my hand. She smiled at me. It felt really warm in the cool desert morning. The smile, I mean. I smiled back at her.

"You know what?" she said. "It's really great to see you again."

I felt the same way.

Geomancy

JANE WAS STILL fast asleep in the back seat as we left Rhesus. I briefly glanced at Max's directions, then handed them to Terry. She studied them a moment.

"What kind of directions are these?" She looked up at me.

"Feng shui," I said.

"You guys have a hard time being normal," she concluded.

Max's directions were riddled with Feng Shui, the ancient Chinese art of placement. It was a form of geomancy, concerned with the flow of life-force energy depending on the lay of the land, vegetation, structures, the shape of structures and rooms, the placement of furniture, the use of color and so on. Max knew I was deeply interested in the practice and had framed his directions around the Feng Shui interpretation of the landscape as well as a quote from Lin Yutang, depicting the perfect placement of a home.

"By the side of the house there is a road and the road must branch off," Terry read. "At the point where several roads come together, there is a bridge, and the bridge must

be tantalizing to cross. At the end of the bridge there are
trees and the trees must be tall. In the shade of the trees
there is grass, and the grass must be green. Above the grass
plot there is a ditch, and the ditch must be slender. At the
top of the ditch there is a spring, and the spring must gurgle. Above the spring there is a hill, and the hill must be
deep." She paused at the next clue. "Between the azure
dragon, the white tiger and the black tortoise."

That was the clue I needed. There were several roads
out of town. I turned on the one that headed towards the
hills, for that is where I would find the dragon, the tiger
and the tortoise. It was a Feng Shui description of a perfect
location for a home, in the "armchair" created by three hills,
one behind and another on each side, protecting the house
from too much weather and too much sun.

The road soon turned and followed the gentle contours
of the foothills. At an intersection, I stopped the Jeep, considering which way the clues led. Terry studied the directions some more.

"We probably have to read them backwards," I told her.

"Then we need a 'deep hill'," she said.

Studying the landscape, one hill in particular seemed like
it might fit that description. It stood tall, separate from the
'body of the dragon' as the main mass of a range of hills is
called. Its sides were steep and broad. Deep might be a
good word for it. I turned that way.

The road climbed up towards the base of the hill. As we
passed behind it, a stream joined the road, flowing gently
alongside.

"There's our ditch," I guessed aloud.

"Then we're looking for trees and a bridge." Terry peered through the windshield, looking ahead. "Look! There!"

Sure enough, we could see a grove of trees in the distance. Beside them was a bridge, crossing the stream. And as the Jeep rumbled across the bridge, we came to a crossroads where several roads came together.

"Now which way?" Terry wondered.

"We look for the azure dragon, white tiger and black tortoise."

I took the road which seemed to go uphill. The clues were relatively easy but fun, if you knew the Feng Shui. Max did, after all, want me to find him. And soon the armchair configuration came into view. But the road didn't seem to run there. Then around a bend, we came upon a side road which branched off. I took it to below the armchair and pulled over in front of a gate.

"This is it," I guessed. In response to Terry's questioning look, I recited the entire Lin Yutang quote which I had long ago memorized.

"Inside the gate there is a footpath, and the footpath must be winding. At the turning of the footpath there is an outdoor screen, and the screen must be small. Behind the screen there is a terrace, and the terrace must be level. On the banks of the terrace there are flowers, and the flowers must be fresh. Beyond the flowers is a wall, and the wall must be low. By the side of the wall, there is a pine tree and the pine tree must be old. At the foot of the pine tree there are rocks, and the rocks must be quaint. Over the rocks there is a pavilion, and the pavilion must be simple. Behind the pavilion are bamboos, and the bamboos must be thin and sparse. At the end of the bamboos there is a house, and the house must be secluded. By the side of the house there is a road and the road must branch off. At the point where several roads come together, there is a bridge, and the bridge must be tantalizing to cross. At the end of the bridge there are trees and the trees must be tall. In the shade of the trees there is grass, and the grass must be green. Above the grass plot there is a ditch, and the ditch must be slender. At the top of the ditch there is a spring, and the spring must gurgle. Above the spring there is a hill, and the hill must be deep. Below the hill there is a hall, and the hall must be square. At the corner of the hall there is a vegetable garden, and the vegetable garden must be big. In the vegetable garden there is a stork, and the stork must dance. The stork announces that there is a guest, and the guest must not be vulgar. When the guest arrives there is wine, and wine must not be declined. During the service of the wine, there is merriment, and the merry guest must not want to go home."

"It's beautiful." The voice came from the back seat. We turned. Jane was sitting up, still pale but looking somewhat rested.

"How are you feeling?" Terry asked.

Jane managed the edge of a smile and looked out the window. "What a beautiful place to throw up." she said.

We got out of the car and walked through the gate, closing it again behind us. I knew we were in the right place. We were quickly swallowed in most of the details of the Lin Yutang scene. We passed a level terrace with mowed grass growing on its top and festooned with flowers on the side, then on the other side of a wall, flanked by a pavilion big enough for a hundred people, open on the sides with a canvas top striped in two shades of green. Further up the path, beyond the sparse bamboos behind the terrace we came across a hall, of course. The eaves were upturned, in the Chinese fashion. I was stunned. He had built Yu-tang's perfect Feng Shui environment. A large vegetable garden spread out to one side. We stopped and stared.

"The son of a bitch actually got a stork for this place," I said.

As we looked at the snow-white bird, it cried out, an-nouncing our presence. Terry, Jane and I looked at one another.

"Um," Jane said slowly, "If I remember the poem right, I think you aren't supposed to be vulgar."

We continued up the path which curved around a stand of trees to reveal a large house, built in the hacienda style. It blended in so perfectly with its surroundings that we scarcely saw it until we were at the steps to the front porch. The three of us stopped and looked up. Max was standing there in sandals, jeans, a sweatshirt and yesterday's five-o'clock shadow. We must have looked shocked because he cracked a huge grin and opened his arms.

"Welcome to Sanctuary, my friends." He leaped off the porch and gave us hugs all around.

He was so full of questions about how I liked his clues and what I thought of the place and what took me so long to get there that we lost track of anything else until a famil-iar voice grabbed our attention.

"What's going on here?" Jennifer, Max's tall, slender girlfriend, stood on the porch. Max always relied heavily on her deep intuition.

"Look who's here, honey," Max said, gesturing grandly in our direction.

But her intuition must have brought her outside on our arrival, interrupting what might have been a more regal welcome.

"Max..." Jennifer pointed to the steps where Jane sat curled in a fetal position.

Max, always a bastion of physical strength, picked her up and carried her into the house. "C'mon in," he called to us.

Terry and I did our greetings with Jennifer and she led us inside. We followed Max up a curved main staircase and into a second floor bedroom. After setting her down, Max turned to us.

"So what's the short version of this story?"

Short versions not being my long suit, I deferred to Terry who ran through Jane's history, reminding Max of Jane's early forays at using his work, continuing through the refusal of another course of chemotherapy then their arrival at my house and our journey here.

"You have to help her," she finished.

"She came to me before and decided that energetic work wasn't what she wanted," he said.

"She changed her mind, Max," Terry said, starting to get that don't-give-me-any-crap-or-I'll-eat-you-alive look.

Max smiled at her resolve. "I'll see what I can do," he said.

Jennifer had listened quietly to Terry's story, sitting beside Jane sleeping on the bed. She tucked a blanket around her and turned to me and Terry. "Why don't I get you two set up with a place to sleep."

"Jen, honey," Max said, "Get Terry set up first. We have something else to do." He signaled me to follow him and we went back down the staircase and crossed the main room to a counter with several stools. He went around the other side of the counter.

There was something different about him, but I couldn't quite put my finger on it. He seemed more relaxed perhaps. He caught me studying him and cracked a big grin.

"So what would you rather have," Max asked. "A fatted calf or a shot of tequila?"

I must have looked confused.

"Let me give you a hint," he said. "You're a vegetarian." He handed me a shot of tequila. "Glad you finally made it." He raised his glass and I raised mine. I laughed. Max still had his fondness for fine tequila. The golden liquid went down like velvet fire. Max filled us up again.

I had a lot of questions for Max, starting with his abrupt departure. But mostly I wanted to hear about the breakthroughs he had mentioned in his letter. Max was a pioneer, another Tesla or Einstein, a genius in his own right. In fact, I thought of him as the high priest of what he did, in the same way that Einstein was the high priest of the religion called physics.

"I took a chance bringing Jane," I said. "I didn't know if it would be all right."

"I've taken a few chances. I've even been right once in a while." Max laughed. "How's your stomach? It should be all better by now."

Time stood still. He couldn't possibly have known how I was feeling on the drive here. Nor could he have known that I was feeling better.

"What are you talking about?" I demanded.

"Your stomach. It should be all better by now."

"How did you know about my stomach?"

Max laughed and said, "We'll get to that later."

"Well, then, how do you know it's better?" I was getting irritated.

"I took care of it," he said.

It wasn't the first time Max's penchant for being cryptic had frustrated me.

"Can you tell me how you did it just in case it happens again and you're not around?" I asked.

"That's why you're here," Max smiled.

"Is this the breakthrough you mentioned in your letter?"

He didn't reply and, at any rate, I knew I wouldn't get any more information from him because he had the annoying habit of preferring to demonstrate his findings, rather than discuss them. But I guessed it wouldn't take very long to get that demonstration.

Jane:
An Energetic Evaluation

JENNIFER AND TERRY went to fetch Jane. They found her slumped in a chair, eyes closed. Terry touched her arm and Jane sat up.

"How're you feeling?" Terry asked her.

"Worse than I look." Jane managed a smile.

"Max wants to check you," Jennifer said. "Are you feeling up to it?"

"It's what I came here for," Jane said, setting her jaw resolutely. "Let's do it."

She was a little shaky as they escorted her to the bright sunny corner room where Max did his work. A large picture window overlooked the mountains on one side and the estate grounds on the other. Jennifer pulled a chair near Max's desk and offered it to Jane. Moments later, Max came in and told us all to get out.

So Jennifer, Terry and I left the room while Max asked Jane privately if she minded having others observe the session. Shortly, Max opened the door and waved us inside.

"Jane has given her permission for you all to witness her evaluation," he said.

He turned to Jane. "You know you don't have to."

She shrugged. "I'm already public property. Everybody knows I have cancer and if they don't believe it they can see my shiny head." She shifted her wig irreverently.

He sat in the utilitarian chair on the other side of the desk from Jane. Beside him was a computer monitor and on the desk there were a few familiar objects like a computer keyboard and mouse. Then there were some unfamiliar objects. These included a shiny cylinder of polished metal about four inches long and three-quarters of an inch in diameter with a wire running from one end to a plate of brushed aluminum about four inches square. Another wire ran from the aluminum plate to a black box with a couple of switches and a dial on it. A third wire ran from the black box to a probe with a blunt brass point and a black insulated handle. A heavy plug led a fourth, thicker wire down to the computer. Finally there was a covered bowl full of cotton balls and a container of rubbing alcohol.

Max looked at Jane without speaking for a moment, as if he was trying to decide something.

"I have to know one thing," he finally announced. "What are you here for?"

Jane looked at Terry, then me, then Jennifer, as if we could provide an answer.

"I'm asking *you*, Jane," Max said.

"I want you to cure me," she said. "I know — it's the wrong answer, you don't cure anything."

"Right."

"So do whatever it is you do."

Looking at Max and Jane was a study in contrasts. He was vital and strong and she was frail and weak. But despite her ailments, she was still stubborn and fiery.

"I balance subtle energies in the body," Max said. "I don't even know yet whether this will help you. The bad news is that it doesn't help some people, but I'll know very quickly whether that's the case with you. It's my first question. The good news is that it does help most people. But I'm not going to find disease, per se. That requires lab tests and other diagnostic procedures that have nothing to do with *my* work. Commonly, I use words that sound like the names of diseases, but I'm using those words to describe frequencies that are commonly associated with disease, but are not proven to be the actual diseases themselves."

"Associated by who?" Jane asked.

"Other people who have done work in this field," Max said. "I did not invent the concept of energetic balancing, but to my knowledge there is nobody else who can do it. There are many theorists out there and they have researched the field heavily, but they are missing an essential element which I have discovered."

"But if you can't find the actual diseases, what difference does it make?"

Jane seemed unsure of herself and I couldn't blame her. Max's model, his paradigm was so substantially different from the physical/material concepts we have all been brought up with that it required a complete re-framing of our knowledge of the world. The trick, of course, is that what he does actually works. Without that, the whole thing would be the empty posturing of an academic. Unfortunately, this was and is the case with the majority of energetic approaches people promote.

"Jane, *all* life is energetic," Max said. "I didn't discover that, it's taught in every high school. In the view of modern physics, the world, the entire universe in fact, is simply energy. Your life is a subset of the entire universe. Therefore, you are simply energy. If you are willing to believe the scientists who tell us that, then what I do makes sense. These scientists include Einstein, Bohr, Heisenberg and many others who have spent their lives trying to understand the subtle invisible forces that make up the world. Your life, your eyelash, your altered nose, your cancer, your hope, your despair, and even your current confusion are made up of measurable and changeable energetic frequencies.

"But the bottom line is: Can I make a change in your well-being?"

Max got a mischievous look on his face and paused for what I could only construe as dramatic impact.

"The answer," he drawled slowly, "is *no*, I can't."

I felt confused myself at that moment and I could see by their faces that Jane and Terry were going through the same thing. Jennifer, on the other hand, was sharing a conspiratorial look with Max, so I knew there was some kind of set-up going on.

"You can't?" Jane asked.

"Nope," Max deadpanned.

"If you can't change anything, why am I even here?"

"*I* can't change anything," Max said, "but *you* can."

"I can?" Jane repeated dully.

"You can. The work I do brings your inner subtle-energy forces into balance so that your own self-organizing principle brings your body, your mind, your emotions and even your spiritual self back into a state of well-being. That's one of the reasons not everybody can benefit from this. Because you yourself are the motivating force of this work, you must have enough energy, enough personal power, to bring yourself back to an optimum state after your energies have been brought into balance. In my experience, even many people who are very weak still have enough energy for this, but there are some who cannot do it. But this force can be measured and we'll know as soon as we begin whether this is the case for you."

Jane pondered his words, staring off into space for a moment. Then she looked at him.

"Can we just get started?" she said. "I don't care about the theory, I just want to get better."

Max tapped a few keys on the keyboard and the monitor on his desk sprang to life. He wet down a paper towel with a small spray bottle, wrapped it around the shiny cylindrical electrode and handed it to Jane.

"Hold this in your left hand."

She took the object and gripped it tightly.

"Not too firmly," Max told her. "Just so it doesn't escape."

Max picked up the brass-tipped probe and a cotton ball which he doused with alcohol. He took her right hand and wiped the side of her thumb with the cotton ball.

"Why are you doing that?" Jane asked.

"This removes oils from your skin so we make a good contact with the probe. The other probe has a wet paper towel on it for the same reason. Basically it promotes electrical conductivity."

Max punched some keys and the monitor flipped through a few lists. He selected one and a grid came on the screen. It was about six squares wide and eight squares high. In each square was a cryptic abbreviation, indicating a name for some energetic imbalance. He pressed a button and all the squares became highlighted on the monitor. Then he pressed the probe to her thumb and a meter-like bar rose on one side of the screen as an accompanying whine came from the computer's speaker. The pitch went up as the bar went up. He adjusted a dial on the black box and again pressed Jane's thumb with the probe. He seemed satisfied with his calibration.

"Do you know if I can be helped yet?" Jane questioned.

"Not yet," he said. "But we'll know soon."

Max immediately went to a page and isolated a box which elicited a high-pitched sound when he pressed the probe to her thumb. He looked at Jane.

"Good news," he said. "You have nothing that cannot be reversed."

"You mean my cancer?" she asked.

"I don't know yet if you have the *frequency* for cancer," Max told her, "let alone the disease. So far, I just know that whatever you have can be changed."

He moved to another box and pressed the probe to her thumb again. He got a low-pitched whine this time. He looked up.

"Her life force is low," he said.

It seemed redundant, considering her appearance.

"But," he continued to himself, "it can be increased."

He selected another box, tested again and said to Jane, "You have a frequency which has the potential to end your life shortly."

"You mean the cancer," she said with finality.

"I've already answered that," Max replied.

Another test.

"Whatever you have is getting worse," Max said.

"It's getting close to sea-level," Jane replied cryptically.

He then went to another page and said, "Let's measure her *exact* life force."

More boxes, more tests. He raised his head from the screen and her thumb. "Your life force is acceptable to work with — but barely."

This news didn't seem like much relief to Jane who hung on every word, not sure whether to believe him or not. I pulled my chair closer and put a comforting hand on her shoulder.

"Don't touch her," Jennifer said. "We don't want a group frequency."

I was abashed. I actually knew better. Max had long ago demonstrated to me that when people touch, their energetic essence intermingles, causing changes in their frequencies. He had once had me rest a hand on my girlfriend while he tested her and demonstrated that she had an inflamed prostate which, happily, I knew was impossible.

"Now let's see what's wrong with you," Max said to Jane. "Do you have the frequency of cancer?" He held up a finger to her, to prevent her replying.

To answer his own question, he paged through some screens on the computer. He stopped at one labeled "Malignancy Frequencies" and pressed a key which highlighted all the boxes on that screen. He touched the probe to Jane's thumb. A low-pitched whine indicated a "hit."

"What's that?" Jane asked.

"You have one of the frequencies on this screen," Max said.

He began isolating the boxes, first by highlighting the upper half of the screen. He pressed the probe to her thumb. The high-pitched whine indicated that the frequency wasn't in the upper half of the screen. He moved to the top two lines of the bottom half of the screen and tested again. In this methodical way, he continued until he isolated a single box which indicated the specific imbalance.

"You have the frequency of cancer," he said. "of the thyroid."

Jane just looked. Max continued testing.

"Breast... lung... and brain." More testing. "It's in the bone."

Jane said, "It's everywhere. It's hopeless."

Max looked at her and said, "We already saw these frequencies can be reversed. I wouldn't continue testing you if they couldn't."

"Does it say it's in my uterus?" Jane peered fearfully at the screen.

"If it is, it's hiding." Max replied. "Let's see." He flipped through screens, pressed buttons, pushed the probe against her thumb time and again.

"There it is," he pointed at the screen. "It doesn't want to be found."

His words jolted her. "*It* doesn't *want* to be found?" she echoed, incredulous.

"The frequency is hiding," Max said, matter-of-factly. "It's disguised."

Ignoring Jane's open mouth, he turned back to the machine. "Let's strip the disguise away." More screens, more testing. "Yes, it's in the uterus." More testing. "And the intestine."

"Okay," Max turned to Jane, "let's see what else you have."

He spent the next twenty minutes running the machine through hundreds of trays.

"Nothing else significant," Max said. "Just the obligatory TB."

"I have cancer and tuberculosis?" Jane asked.

"The frequencies," Max smiled. "The frequency of TB is ubiquitous. Almost everyone has it."

"Isn't TB a dangerous disease?" Jane asked.

"Of course," Max replied. "But remember I'm talking about the frequency of TB."

"Is the frequency of TB a dangerous disease?" Jane pressed.

Max raised his eyebrows at her. "It'll be gone in a week," he said. "Is that what you want to know?"

"Until I was diagnosed with cancer, I was healthy as a horse," Jane lamented. "I never got sick, ever."

"People with cancer always say that," Max told her. "What I have found is that if a negative frequency is strong enough it dominates the entire body. It's territorial, like a street gang. It doesn't allow any other frequencies in. Except," he smiled, "TB. Nothing seems to stop that."

Returning to the machine, Max changed some settings. "Let's see where you got this."

Jane looked at him blankly.

"This much malignancy has to have a hereditary base," Max said.

"Neither of my parents had cancer," Jane objected.

"Are they still alive?"

"No, they were killed in a car crash when I was a child."

Max was silent for a moment, then he put his hand on hers. "I don't think you inherited the frequency of the car crash."

He resumed testing.

"There's one," he said. More buttons. "It came from your father. Any others?"

"How would I know?" Jane replied.

"I'm asking your thumb," Max explained.

Jane's thumb slowly revealed two other hereditary malignancy frequencies, again from her father.

"Who cares what my father had?" Jane asked.

Max ignored her and continued. "There they are," he said. "The two frequencies for immune factors that set up a template for the frequency of malignancy."

"Can we get rid of them?" Jane worried.

"It takes about a month," Max told her, putting down the probe and pressing the print button on the computer. The printer spooled out a list of the frequencies he had found.

Jane scanned the paper. "Aren't these diseases? You use the names of diseases."

Max patiently reiterated his position: "Disease is identified by doctors and laboratories by corroborating symptoms as well as through identification of a disease organism or pathogen or an antibody produced by exposure to a pathogen. I don't identify disease. I identify energetic imbalances."

"Then why do you use disease names?" Jane asked.

"Think of these names as another language that sounds like English or medical terms, but isn't," Max said. "Like legalese is to English. The trap in law is that many words are defined not by their common usage but by precedent in the court system. Unfortunately, many of these words are common words that have a different meaning to a lawyer than they do to a lay person. This is also true here. These are names that the medical profession uses to describe specific and verifiable conditions. But when I use these names,

I am referring to an energetic imbalance. I have no proof that the energetic imbalance and the physical thing identified by doctors are the same, thus I make no claims to that effect.

"For more than a hundred years, homeopaths have used terminologies similar to that of medicine without claiming that there is a direct correlation between the words and the diseases. For instance, they often use *tuberculinum* or *streptococcinum* or *carcinominum* as remedies for patients who have presented a set of symptoms that correspond to those associated with that remedy in their textbooks. These remedies contain the *actual diseases*, which are used as treatments without ever suggesting the patient suffered from that disease. Their theory is only stating that an incredibly small amount of that disease would remove the symptoms. Maybe this will make it even more apparent: Imagine that the homeopath decides the appropriate remedy is *rhus tox*. This doesn't suggest the patient has poison ivy. Or if the homeopath uses *sepia*, which is cuttlefish ink, it doesn't suggest the patient is really a squid. *Lachesis*, the venom of a bushmaster, might be used, not because the patient is suffering from snake bite, but because of the classical association between that remedy and the set of symptoms. I accept the principles of homeopathy but I've taken them to another level. I do not use any physical agent, only the subtle-energy frequencies that I find associated with a set of symptoms. But even *that* I've taken to another level — because I don't look for symptoms, I look for subtle-energy imbalances."

"So this is homeopathy?" Jane asked.

"No," Max said, "because I don't use homeopathic remedies or homeopathic diagnostic techniques."

"Then what do I call you?" she wondered.

"Why not 'Max, the energetic practitioner,'" Max smiled. "Unless you're more comfortable with something that sounds more familiar. If an MD is an allopath, how about calling me an 'energypath' or 'frequencypath' or 'electropath?'"

She shrugged.

"How about 'idiopath?'" I interjected, "since what you do is unknown." The word "idiopathic" is a word used by doctors to mean "of unknown origin."

"Take any 'path' you like," he laughed. "They all lead to Sanctuary."

She waited. Max continued.

"Jane, I understood you had a medically-diagnosed cancer when you first called me and I told you I didn't treat cancer or any other disease. You may think I'm trying to avoid answering you. I'm not. I'm avoiding making a claim I can't substantiate. If that lowers your hopes, I'm sorry about that. But it is both illegal and unethical for me to claim *anything* that I can't substantiate and demonstrate. Understand, though I'm entitled to my beliefs, I can't offer them as facts. And I never try to *persuade* anyone to accept my beliefs as facts. That's precisely why, for years, both as a doctor and a consultant, not only did I avoid advertising or soliciting patients or clients, I would not even take someone for an energetic evaluation unless they were referred by a client of mine who they knew personally. If my client felt he or she had benefited from my energetic work, fine. They're free to say whatever they want. I'm not. And I do not and will not. Perhaps someday it will turn out that the energetic footprint of something *is* that thing. Perhaps not. But I guess you can say 'perhaps' or 'perhaps not' about anything. When my work conforms to their standards of diagnosis and *they* say it's the same, then it's the same. Until then, it is not the same, and I will not violate any legal or ethical consideration. And, frankly, I don't think it *is* the same. I believe it's a greater, but different, issue. If *you* need to say it's the same, feel free to do what you want. If you need *me* to say it, I can't help you and won't attempt to do so. Your insistence is futile. All I can end up doing is asking you to please leave."

"But what about all the people who say you've helped them?" Jane asked.

"When I say I don't deal with disease, it doesn't mean my work has no value," Max replied. "I can honestly tell you I've never destroyed one germ. That doesn't mean my clients have not overcome their diseases. The aim of energetic balancing is to give the body enough strength, which I call 'energy,' to use its own wisdom and its own resources to provide a state of well-being."

"Like spontaneous remission?" Jane asked.

"The concept of spontaneous remission is totally consistent with current medical terminology," he agreed. "Investigating and implementing that concept has some relationship to my work. Killing germs has never been my field. That belongs to another profession."

"People see you, then go back to their doctors and find that their diseases have gone away." Jane insisted.

"Nothing happens without a reason," Max replied. "Spontaneous healing does not mean 'random' or 'accidental' or 'incidental' healing. It means the reason for the healing is unknown, which is quite different from 'non-existent.' If my work lets you use your energy to fight your disease, it is you, not me, who succeeds or fails in that fight. As an example, let's say I suggested drinking more orange juice and you got fewer colds, would you say I cured your cold? Of course not."

She nodded, understanding.

"You already know that there is an innate self-organizing principle in your body whose purpose is to maintain health," Max continued. "If that organization is disrupted, your ability to resist or overcome infections is hampered or lost. If you need a term for what I am doing, let's say I am organizing you to help you deal with your specific problems. If I succeed, it's highly possible you will go back to your doctor and be found free of your diseases." He paused and looked at her. "Because," he continued, "*you* will have overcome them."

"Spontaneously?" Jane asked.

"Your doctor might think so," Max replied, "because it didn't come about as the result of anyone specifically trying to kill a germ. Perhaps that's what they mean by spontaneous. Think about this: Does the term 'spontaneous health' make any sense?"

Jane didn't reply.

"The answer is 'Of course,'" Max continued. "What other kind of health is there? How does your doctor know whether or not he has overcome malignant cells in himself countless times? He'll only know about it when he doesn't overcome them. What about diseases that are considered fatal one-hundred percent of the time, but which are only diagnosable in an autopsy? If you can't identify a disease in a living subject, how can you say that the disease is always fatal? You can only say that it has only been identified in dead people. Living people may routinely overcome these dread diseases — *if* they have the energetic integrity, the health-generating self-organization, to do so."

Jane took in what he was saying. "So how is what you do different from what doctors do?"

"You've just watched what I do and how I do it," he went on. "You watched quite carefully, in fact."

Jane nodded her agreement.

"Did I ever ask you about symptoms?" Max asked.

"No."

"Did I take any tissue samples, or blood?"

"No."

"Did I take your blood pressure or measure your pulse? Did I do any kind of physical examination other than lay my eyes on you as you sat across the desk from me?"

"No."

"There it is, then. Maybe the question you should ask is 'How is what I do the *same* as what doctors do?' The answer is that in no way is it the same. None of the things that might be construed as medical examination were performed. In addition, I told you up front that what I do isn't medicine. You're having a small problem with terminology." Max thought for a moment. "Imagine what it was like when people first tried to talk about electricity or the atom. They were describing a world in which things didn't have names. In addition, the things they were describing had no exact corollary in the world of normal experience. That's the way it is with subtle energy now. There was a time when oxygen was called de-phlogistonized air. Nobody today even knows what that means. Right now, the work that I do is struggling for the right words." He paused. "Or maybe *they* aren't using the words correctly. But it doesn't matter either way. My work is mine and theirs is theirs. They have nothing to do with one another, regardless of the chosen terminology."

"Do I have to believe in what you're doing?" Jane asked, obviously wearing down.

"No reasonable person would," he told her. "But then, George Bernard Shaw said 'The reasonable man adapts himself to the world: the unreasonable one persists in trying to adapt the world to himself. Therefore all progress depends on the unreasonable man.'"

She was silent.

"That's why your being here is an act of faith," he concluded.

"Is the work of Sanctuary dependent on faith?" she reiterated.

"Well, Jane, everyone who uses this technology is a believer," he answered. "On the other hand, most of them didn't believe in it until it worked for them."

The room seemed to collectively nod agreement.

"Okay," Jane said. "I'm tired, I can't think anymore."

"All I need is your thumb," Max said.

Jennifer brought over a pillow and put it on the desk. Jane immediately put her head down and shut her eyes.

"Now let's see how we deal with this," Max said. He referred to his printout. "Okay, here's what we found. Let's verify it."

He typed away for a minute, going through a number of screens, highlighting frequencies one at a time, checking each against Jane's thumb. Mumbling agreement with himself as he worked, he quickly went through the list. Each one produced the characteristic low-pitched whine that indicated a hit. "All positive," he said. "Now, let's see what happens if we put this in the circuit."

Max pressed a key, then tested Jane's thumb again. The machine produced a high-pitched noise. "Perfect," he said. "All the malignancy frequencies are negative."

Jane's eyes opened and her head came off the pillow. "You mean it's gone now?" she said. "You just got rid of it?"

"No," Max laughed, "I just showed that I can. What I did was add these frequencies to your circuit and then ask if the malignancy frequencies are still positive in the presence of the balancing frequencies. And the answer is no. Now all we've got to do is get these frequencies into you."

"How do we do that?" Jane asked.

"That's not my department," Max smiled, "so I'll turn you over to the attractive part of the staff."

Jennifer helped Jane up and guided her to the other desk in the office. It contained a computer similar to the one Max used, but there were no probes for testing. As Jane settled down, now fully awake, Jennifer pulled some bottles out of a cabinet in a corner of the office and set them down on the desk. The bottles were sealed. I could see the labels. They read "Energetic Imprinting Solution." The ingredients were listed as alcohol, water and diatomaceous earth.

Jennifer placed each bottle on metal plates which were wired to the computer. Then she turned to the computer and ran through each of the screens Max had found imbalances on. A few moments and key clicks later she had produced several pages which contained Jane's imbalances as well as the frequencies Max found to be effective against them. She pressed a button and a countdown began on the top of the screen. At the same time, a small red LED light on the black box began blinking.

"The computer is charging the bottles on the plate with the energies required to neutralize the imbalances Max found," Jennifer said.

"Why do I have to have a number of different bottles?" Jane asked.

"Some frequencies can't be combined in the same bottle," Jennifer replied, "so we're often required to put them into several bottles."

"What do I do with the bottles?" Jane asked him.

"Each bottle has a dropper and you put a certain number of drops under your tongue. You'll be getting several bottles. Some of them are for acute imbalances which are affecting your immediate sense of well-being. Those bottles require administration of ten drops three times per day for four to seven days. Other bottles are for hereditary imbalances. You'll take three drops from one bottle one night before bed, then three drops from the next bottle the next night. After you finish a round of all the bottles, you start over again with the first one. You have three bottles for hereditary imbalance so every fourth night you'll start the cycle again."

Jane turned to Max. "I don't really understand the hereditary part."

"Conventional medicine recognizes that illnesses can be transmitted genetically. They are starting to identify certain genes that carry some diseases. In my work, I recognize that energetic imbalances can be transmitted hereditarily as well. I believe that this information isn't actually transmitted in the genes, but in a more subtle part of the anatomy.

"There are people who believe that there is more to the human being than a physical body. I am one of them," Max continued. "Mystics say that there are other bodies: the causal body, the mental body, the energetic body, the spirit, etc. They are referred to as the 'subtle bodies' and some people have written about the anatomy of the subtle bodies. For instance, the Yoga Sutras, written five hundred years before Christ by the sage Patanjali, indicate that there are energetic pathways in these subtle bodies and possibly other anatomical features, if you can properly apply the word 'anatomy' to something which is not physical. My work seems to indicate that energetic imbalances are transmitted through these subtle bodies. They can be passed on through many generations if not released. Often, families have common patterns of problems which plague each generation. These include imbalances which may affect the kidneys or the stomach or the brain or the spinal cord. These imbalances allow the body to get out of sync with its own processes and sometimes result in a family pattern of early heart attack deaths or cancer, for instance. The frequency we call hereditary tuberculosis may manifest itself in low energy levels and a tendency to sweat a lot because the hereditary tuberculosis frequency affects the kidneys and doesn't allow them to properly maintain fluid pressures in the body, so the body eliminates excess fluid through the skin. Regardless of the symptomatology, though, the energetic balances can be resolved and, when they are, my clients typically experience exceptional improvements in their sense of well-being."

Max paused and grinned. "Some of my clients have called me the karma doctor because the work I do seems to release them from the 'sins of the father' syndrome where they repeat the same kinds of patterns they have seen in their families. This extends into things like behavior and mood because when a person achieves a state of energetic balance, the things which cause behavior and mood to fluctuate wildly go away and their sense of self and of self-esteem may improve dramatically. People find that many of the things they have come to accept as harsh facts of life are in fact energetic disturbances which can be easily erased."

"I don't understand," Jane said.

"If you think about it, just what it is about you that might have been preordained, that might have been inevitable? Can the inevitable be changed — or is that a contradiction? What do you think you really remember about everything that's formed you?" Max asked.

Jane answered, "I can remember being an infant wanting my mother's —"

Max interrupted, "No! *Really* remember, and not just in this lifetime. This whole process has to do with making you conscious. You think you don't remember your father's cancer frequency — but you really do. I can't read anything that doesn't already exist in you. Where in you does it exist then? Is it in your mind? In your DNA? Is it in some subtle body that the Western world doesn't acknowledge, but is considered a real anatomical entity in other cultures?"

He paused. Jane was speechless.

"The process we are doing here," he continued, "is about helping you know what you already know, that which is already contained within you. But I must warn you: Once you know something consciously you're responsible for it. You're removing your innocence. But I think your own appearance here is proof enough that ignorance is not really bliss."

"So my father had the frequency of cancer," Jane said. "You're saying that affects who I am? I'm not sure I believe it. I mean, his frequency of cancer isn't my personality."

"It isn't?" Max asked. "Do you think having that frequency doesn't shape your personality? Let me ask you — do negative emotions affect you?"

"I guess so," Jane answered. "That's all I have these days."

"Do you think the frequency of cancer is any less likely to have an impact on your personality than the frequency of a negative emotion?" Max continued. "Don't you think carrying this frequency is a weight, a burden? It's like watching a German shepherd with congenital hip dysplasia. First, he favors it. Over time, he adapts to it until he becomes a three-legged dog. Are you going to say his disease didn't affect him? He's not even the same dog by then."

A light bulb turned on in Jane's head.

"So if it *can* have an impact — and some part of you knows that it *does* — wouldn't that affect what you think of as the basic *you*?" Max finished.

"What part of me knows this?" Jane asked.

"Your thumb, for starters," Max laughed.

"Isn't there a basic me?" Jane asked.

"I'm sure there is," Max answered, "but you won't have a clue about it until you're cleaned up at every level. You've spent your entire life getting filthy — contaminated by an oddball assortment of negatives. And as a matter of fact, so have your ancestors — or would you prefer to say your past lives? The terminology doesn't matter much. What does matter is what has it done to you, what is it doing to you now and what will it do to your successors? You can call your physical contamination malignancy. Don't you think there's the equivalent in your personality or your psyche or your energetic body?"

Terry turned to me. "I know exactly what he means," she said. "When I first met you, before you started going to Max, you were very hard to be with, but now I'm feeling... um, you're different, I guess. Better."

"Why are you so sure *he's* the only one who's changed, Terry?" Max questioned. "Except for the fear and anger and self-loathing you used to have — which accompanied your own imbalances — you're exactly the same woman you've always been."

Terry blushed.

"These are ready," Jennifer spoke up. She slid a set of bottles across the desk to Jane.

"When do I start?" she asked.

"I think immediately would be appropriate," Max told her.

Jane examined the bottles, each with a different code scribbled on it.

Jennifer picked one up and began to repeat the now-familiar ritual. "Let me show you," she said. "You have to activate the energy in them before you take them by doing this." She whacked the bottle sharply a few times against the heel of her hand. Then she took out the dropper, filled it almost halfway. "About ten drops. Open up." She squirted it under Jane's tongue. "Keep it there for a minute before you swallow."

We all sat watching her until finally Jane said, "What am I supposed to feel?"

"I don't know exactly," Max said, "but whatever it is you probably won't like it at first. These frequencies are going to come out and they may come out kicking."

"Kicking?" she said.

"Holding on to these frequencies is a form of suppression," Max replied. "Energetic balancing takes you through a process which brings whatever you suppressed to the surface — *your* surface, your consciousness. You'll experience each of these frequencies in the way you needed to in the first place. Once you've experienced them, you can let them go. This is especially true of the hereditary frequencies. That's why you take them at night. But at night, while you may not experience direct physical discomfort, the hereditary frequencies often cause vivid dreams, not always pleasant."

"I'm an expert at discomfort," Jane said. "I've done chemo."

Max nodded in acknowledgement.

"I understand you're going to be staying with us for a while," Jennifer said.

"I don't have anything better to do," Jane said. "Other than return to Los Angeles and wait to die. I can do that anywhere. My office can do without me in the meantime."

"We'll check you again in a few days," Max said. "Just to be sure it's working."

"How will you know?" Jane asked, overwhelmed by it all.

Max smiled. "You'll tell me."

"You mean my thumb?" Jane asked.

"Hopefully with more than that," he told her.

Her first session with Max was over.

Max and Me

LATER that evening, Max and I walked through Sanctuary. We walked silently until he turned to me and asked, "You don't understand what this is, do you?"

"A great hangout?" I guessed.

"It's the end of an era," he said.

I felt confusion. "What are you talking about? You've just built the place."

"This place represents an ideal based on a consciousness whose time is past."

"Ecological ideals?" I asked, incredulous.

"Not just that," Max said. "Ideals about the physical world, about materialism. Or to put it another way: It represents a time when we believed in a perfect world that was physical. Now, as a representation or culmination of that ideal, it becomes a jumping-off place into a new world view. It's no accident that this is a time when there is so much excitement about virtual worlds and cyberspace," he concluded.

I knew what he meant, in a way. It seemed as if more and more, life was about abstracts. Representational art had long been passé, only conceptual art seemed to garner attention. Economics was about business models, instead of products and sales. Wealth was about the perception of abundance, rather than the accumulation of assets. People spent more time creating and enjoying their own little world in their homes because instinctively they knew that the world that they created was their reality. Meanwhile, people who stayed stuck in the older economic model, based on physical work and working with the physical world, found it harder to survive. I relayed this to Max to see if we were on the same wavelength.

"Exactly," he said, seeming satisfied that I was hearing him. "Which brings us to what my work is really about: It's about transcending limitations, transcending old models. On a gross vibrational level, it's about transcending the limits of our physical bodies. You've seen it yourself time and time again."

"You're implying that there's somewhere else to go," I said.

"You've always challenged me about why I don't consider what I do to be medicine," he said. "Of course, you know that I don't use any medical techniques or claim that what I do has anything to do with the physical body. So that begs the question what it does have to do with."

I waited for him to answer his own question.

He spoke slowly and carefully: "It has to do with becoming more conscious. It has to do with spiritual awakening. It has to do with making the transition from vibrating at a lower level on a physical plane to vibrating at a higher level on an energetic plane."

I didn't say anything because I was trying to put this information together with what I already knew of his work. Max had always said that the things he did in his energetic consulting practice was merely the tip of the iceberg.

"The possibilities for energetic balancing are endless. As we eliminate each imbalance, it increases the energy we have available to us. This creates the opportunity to discover deeper, more subtle imbalances, until..." he hesitated.

"Until what?" I was intrigued.

"Until we are free from the limitations we're acquired in this lifetime and in the past," he continued. "I believe that's called transcending karma — which is your destiny."

We had crossed the terrace and stopped in front of the large hall with its upturned eaves painted red.

Max nudged me. "Follow me." He opened the door into the pavilion and we stepped inside.

Light poured in through the large windows. Three rows of four desks filled the room. On each desk was a computer and energetic testing equipment. There was one chair on each side of each desk.

"This is the beginning," Max said.

"The beginning of what? A frequency data-processing department?"

"I'll show you."

He crossed to one of the desks and sat down, motioning me to sit opposite him.

"Turn on the computer."

I flipped the switches and while we waited for the machine to load its software I handed him the brass-tipped testing probe, suddenly conscious that I was on the wrong side of the desk — the operator's side. He pointed at me.

"You do it," he said, grabbing the polished cylindrical grounding electrode.

"Me?" I heard myself say in a shrill voice. "I don't know how."

"Try it," he said. "You've seen me do it enough times."

So I navigated to the testing screens using the computer keyboard, then clumsily imitated the movements I had watched him make, wiping his thumb with an alcohol-soaked cotton ball and pressing the probe to the spot I thought it might be. To my surprise and pleasure, I got a reading! After several tries, I moved to the next screen and tested again. Max coached me a little bit on technique and I modified my approach per his advice. Within a short time, I came up with several frequency imbalances in Max, thanks to his careful coaching and interpretation of the machine's reaction to my awkward technique.

When I looked up from his thumb and the computer screen, Max was smiling.

"You did it," he said. "That's one of the break-throughs."

"Other people can do it?" I asked.

"Other people can be trained to do the testing," he confirmed. "You're a bit faster than most, because you already knew how to run the software. And you need more training, of course; you're not quite ready for prime time, as they say. But I can test people for their ability to do energetic balancing, so I'll know who to train. Let me ask you something: How many people need what I do?"

"All of them," I said, "as far as I know."

"Exactly. The potential is unlimited because almost everyone needs this. We live in an age where people are waking up to the possibilities of energy. After a hundred years of applied electricity and the evolution of thought in electronics and physics, people have started to make the connections between religious concepts and the way the world actually works. In other words, the idea that everything is made of energy is starting to manifest itself in more and more areas of our lives. What my work has done is apply the concepts of energy to the elusive goal of human potential. Millions of people are ready for it. They've come to the point where they know that the Golden Rule — do unto others as you would have them do unto you — works because E does equal mc-squared.

"So now it will be available to everybody?" I asked.

"Not now, but soon," he said. "First, I've got to clone myself. That's the first goal of Sanctuary. Because without that how do all these people find out that this is available? And if they do find out, who will test them? Working at my maximum level, seven days a week, there are already thousands of people who want me to do energetic balancing for them. But I can't accommodate all of them."

"No question," I said. "You were overworked in Los Angeles. I saw you chained to your computer."

"It doesn't have to be just me anymore," he said quietly.

Max got up and opened a cabinet. He rummaged inside for a moment.

"There's yet another part to this equation," he said, sitting back down again. "Switch with me." He handed me the cylindrical grounding electrode and took the brass-tipped probe. He tossed a stack of photographs on the desk. Most of them were polaroids but some were regular prints. He flipped through them until he came up with a picture of a sickly-looking middle-aged woman.

He held up the picture. "Watch closely."

He put the picture down on the metal plate attached to the wire connecting the shiny cylinder in my left hand with the black box on the table. He grabbed my right hand and pressed the probe to my thumb.

The sequence of hits led us to the cancer-frequency tray. (Tray is the term Max used to refer to a given screenful of information.) Another few presses on the thumb along with the appropriate refocusing of the range covered by each inquiry took us to the frequency of ovarian carcinoma.

I was appalled. "Does this mean I have cancer?" I asked worriedly.

Max looked up at me, exasperated. "Aren't you concerned about having an ovary?"

"But I don't have an ovary, Max." I looked at him like he was nuts.

"Here," Max said. "Let's first resolve your sexual conflict."

He flipped to a page where the frequencies for "male" and "female" were available. He tested and the machine indicated "female." He took the picture off the plate and tested again. It came up with "male." He put the picture back on and tested again. Female, again. Apparently the machine could distinguish that another person, the person in the photograph, was being tested.

"Now let's deal with your cognitive dissonance," he said

He took the woman's picture off the aluminum plate and grabbed my thumb. He pressed the probe looking for a hit on the cancer-frequency tray. It tested negative. He put the woman's picture back on the plate, then tested again. He got a definite hit.

I was dumbfounded. "I still don't get it."

"What you don't get," Max said, "is that the frequency of an ovary — a cancerous ovary — is in the picture, but not in you."

He took the picture away and tested again. No cancer frequency. He put the picture back and tested another time. The cancer frequency indicated positive again.

I was speechless. What I was witnessing seemed impossible, yet he was repeating the results uniformly.

"If this works," I asked, "why can't you just test the picture, without a person to be a 'thumb?'"

"The technical term is 'witness,'" Max laughed, "but nobody here uses it. The reason we have to have the 'thumb' or 'witness' is because the testing only works on an actual life force. We can replace the 'energetic identity' of the witness with that of the photographic subject, but we cannot make a measurement unless a life-force is present in the testing circuit. Which is why we can't put your picture on a chair and test it by itself. It has an energetic frequency but not a life force."

He fanned out the other photos and picked a few out.

"Let's test some more pictures," Max said.

We ran through tray after tray on each one, finding different energetic imbalances on every picture. I made him check extra carefully, but the results seemed unambiguous. Then, wordlessly, he got up and pulled some written files. The names on the files matched the names on the pictures. They had been checked that day. On each one's files, the energetic imbalances we had just found were already written neatly with today's date.

"They were checked a few hours ago," he said.

"This is a joke or a trick of some sort."

"You've known me too long for me to play games over something this serious," Max replied.

"You're expecting me to believe that a person's photograph is the same as the person when it comes to testing for energetic imbalances?"

"Well," Max ruminated, "I suppose once you accept the possibility of energetic balance as a legitimate approach to achieving well-being, you're already pretty far down the road to accepting the possibility that the entire set of energetic information available in the individual is also available in his or her photograph."

"How can this be?" I moaned in my most plaintive voice, sounding somewhat high and lonely, like a nineteenth-century cowboy somewhere off in the desert who has just seen a space shuttle.

"Before I approach the answer to that question," Max said, "let's look at something else."

He gathered the pictures up and went back over to the cabinet where he got them. He gestured for me to come over and showed me what was inside.

"This is the other part of the equation," Max said.

Inside the cabinet were several more computers. Attached to each computer through one of Max's black boxes were several metal plates. Max started placing the photographs on the plates.

"They're going back where they came from," he said.

On the monitors for each computer in the cabinet was a list of the frequencies we had found. The machines were running imprinting programs just like I'd seen for the bottles so many times over the years.

"This is the same procedure I've watched Jennifer do a million times when she sets up the bottles of drops that you've given me," I said. "You pump the specific balancing energies for any identified imbalance into the bottle when you put the bottle on the plate..."

I stopped, realizing that it wasn't the bottles that were on the plates. It was the pictures.

"As I said earlier," Max continued gently, "once you accept the possibility of energetic balance as a legitimate approach to achieving well-being, you're already pretty far down the road to accepting the possibility that the entire set of energetic information available in the individual is also available in his or her photograph. To push the whole thing a bit further, once you've accepted the possibility that the energetic information associated with the individual can be found in the photograph, it's not that big of a stretch that the opposite is also true."

"The energetic information associated with the photograph can be found in the individual as well?" I ventured, not liking the implications of the whole thing very much at all.

"Exactly," Max said. "Do you remember the associative principle of mathematics?"

His question was an instant trip back to grade school. I hadn't thought about these rules in a millennia or two. "That's where if A equals B, then B equals A," I said, hoping not to be too far off the mark for fourth grade math.

"Correct," Max said. "So if you think about it," he held up a photograph, "if the information in the individual equals the information in the photograph, then the information in the photograph equals the information in the individual."

"Mathematically speaking, I suppose that would be true." I was feeling pretty tentative about this.

"Okay," he nodded. "Now the next question: Is there anything about this energetic information which is not mathematical?"

I didn't have the slightest idea how to answer that question.

"Think harder," he urged. "The energetic information is all represented numerically. So don't the numerical rules apply?"

"I suppose they do," I said grudgingly.

"Exactly!" Max thumped me on the back.

"I am not a photograph," I wailed in my best Elephant Man imitation, "I am a human being!"

Max wasn't amused. "Do you recall," he asked, "that aboriginal 'primitive' people refuse to have their pictures taken because they believe it captures their soul?"

"I've read about it," I replied.

"Every society is primitive in some respect," he said. "It just happens that they're right and we 'moderns' are wrong. As a matter of fact, it captures their exact frequency and the frequency in the photograph changes with them as they change. You probably know that there are people who use pictures to measure the changes in the aura. They get different aura readings over time, using the same picture."

"But I can speak and move, for instance," I pointed out. "My photograph can do neither."

"I never implied that it could," he said.

"So I am not my photograph and my photograph is not me," I concluded.

"Congratulations," Max said. "You've just graduated from the stone age. At this rate, you should be up to the bronze age by the end of the week."

I think I started to get angry right about then. "Look, Max," I found myself yelling, "this isn't reasonable! You can't treat a picture and have the person in it get better!"

"If you're talking about energetic balancing, which isn't really the same as 'treatment,' then you'd be wrong," Max said. "If a photograph contains a person's energetic frequency and you alter the frequency in the photograph, why would you believe you don't alter it in the person?"

"I don't know what to believe," I said, resigned to my confusion.

Max finished setting up the machines to imprint the correct energies into each picture and closed the cabinet.

"We'll see how they do, won't we?" he said.

I was silent.

"Ultimately," Max said, "this entire debate is moot, because the proof is in the implementation. Energetic imbalances *can* be removed in an individual by imprinting that individual's photograph with the frequencies required to remove that imbalance. Remember when you arrived I asked you how your stomach was?"

My blood ran cold as I remembered our arrival — and how queasy I'd been earlier. Max had known before I showed up.

"How did you know I was on my way here?" I demanded.

"I didn't," he told me. "I've been checking you remotely — that's what I call this technique using photos. As a favor. Since I wasn't available for visits. I hope you don't mind."

"Of course not," I replied. I'd been part of Max's inner circle of "lab rats" for a long time. The lab rats had an arrangement with Max that allowed him to freely experiment with his energetic techniques, though I'd always known what he was doing before this.

He pulled out a file and showed it to me. It was mine. He had notes and dates. Pointing some out, he gave me an overview.

"Last Monday, for instance," he said. "You had headaches and felt sluggish, maybe craved sweets."

Dumbly, I nodded.

He offered a few more examples. All of them were correct.

"How long have you been able to use photographs for energetic balancing?" I asked him.

"Quite a while," he replied.

"Why didn't you tell me?"

"It wasn't the right time for you," he said. "But don't feel bad because it wasn't the right time for anybody else either."

I thought about what I had just seen. Max had the ability to do energetic balancing on people using their photographs. The person didn't have to be present for either the energetic evaluation or the subsequent energetic balancing.

"The human body is the most sensitive radio receiver ever made," Max said. "It receives and processes both quantum and analog energies across the entire electromagnetic spectrum, from the lowest possible frequency to the highest, beyond microwave, beyond light, into realms of energy as yet undiscovered or unrecognized by man."

"Since you can balance subtle energy via a person's photograph, do you still need drops at all?" I asked him.

"Sometimes it makes more sense economically," he said. "For instance, hereditary imbalances still take several weeks to a month to remove whether you imprint the photograph or have the person take the imprinted drops. So it makes more sense to take drops rather than tying up the machine for that long, and paying for use of the machine for that period of time. But, yes, you're right, it is possible to not use drops at all," he concluded.

"Do you remember how I made the breakthrough that resulted in the energetic work?" Max asked.

He had told me the story. Years ago he had been an avid desert explorer, spending days or weeks in the remote wildernesses of the southwestern United States. Sometimes he took others with him, but usually he spent the time alone, hiking and climbing, seeking out the places frequented by those who came before us. On one particular trip to the desert, he had climbed to a picturesque remote mountaintop where he planned to camp for the night. While watching the sunset, wathcing the golden light and shadows play across the desert basin below, he found himself hyperaware of his surroundings as if it was part of him. It was as if the changing light was his heartbeat and the wind was the breath in his lungs. He closed his eyes and with his inner vision saw an eagle soar overhead. When he opened his eyes, the eagle was there circling high above him as if protecting him. Suddenly sensing another presence, he turned to find a mountain lion nearby, watching him. When he looked at it, it lay down. With a flap of its great wings, the eagle landed atop a nearby rock. Max was paralyzed, not with fear he said, but with amazement. He looked down at his hand which was clutching a fistful of desert sand. He let it sift slowly back to the ground. And in that moment, watching the hourglass-like flow of sand, made a conceptual connection. In that instant, he saw the solution to the energetic problem he'd been working on: how to measure and affect the subtle energetic essence that mystics had talked about for thousands of years and that Max intuitively knew was connected with electricity and atomic forces.

"I knew at that moment exactly how to achieve my goal," he had told me.

I thumbnailed my recollection for him and he nodded.

"There was another part to that vision," he said. "And that's why we're here now. The eagle and the mountain lion told me I had a duty to bring this work to others and that I would be led to the moment when it could be shared widely. And that it would happen when the time was right. They said there would be a church."

"A church?" I repeated.

"A church of energy," Max said. "You know why this place is called Sanctuary?"

I shook my head.

"Sanctuary is the name for the interior of a church," he told me. "This whole place is a cathedral for *this* church."

He spent the next several hours talking about the church and why he had come out here to start it.

"Spirit is energy," Max said. "And energy is spirit. $E=mc^2$. Energy is in all things, makes up all things. Thus, all illness is spiritual, which is to say all illness is energetic in nature. Dis–ease is due to an individual's misalignment with the power of the spiritual energy which is in them and which is all around them. By realigning the individual to be in harmony with the spiritual force, the life force, the subtle energetic matrix that makes up the entire universe, that individual's physical, emotional and even spiritual ailments will disappear."

"What do you mean by 'energetic matrix?'" I asked.

"Everything that *is*," he said.

He explained a phenomenon called 'virtual photons,' known in esoteric physics. They are a special class of photons which, according to theory, cannot escape the influence of the electron which emits them and thus cannot become ordinary light. Instead they intersect with other virtual photons at the subatomic level to form a matrix of frozen light, a gigantic hologram that *is* the fabric of reality as we know it.

"Information *is* energy," Max said. "I believe the reason Christ could perform miracles was because, as a divine being, he knew this. Where attention goes, energy flows."

"The reason photographs work for energetic testing and subsequent imprinting to achieve balance is that the photograph is a precise alignment of virtual photons which tunnel to the person or thing depicted in it," he explained.

"Tunnel?" I asked. "Through what?"

"Not *through* anything," he replied. "In a sense, through time and space, but at the level of the virtual photon there is no time or space. The tunnel I'm referring to is a word we use to describe the connection."

I couldn't understand everything he said as he went into more obscure scientific detail, but he told me that his work was the bridge between science and spirit.

"Science is a branch of religious thought," Max said. "It is another of man's attempts to explain the universe. This work comes at a time of crisis. Spiritual crisis, psychological crisis, physical crisis." He paused. "Do you believe in miracles?"

"I don't know," I said. "What is a miracle? Unexplained phenomena?"

"Exactly," Max said. "And any technology which is sufficiently advanced becomes indistinguishable from magic. Heinlein said that. So is what I do technology? Or is it magic?"

I didn't know what to answer.

Max answered for me: "It's neither. And it's both. It comes down to this: We can talk about the physics behind what I do, but science can't dissect the mystery at the heart of our existence. Because as soon as you cut it open it disappears. It's as if the mystery only exists if you behold it with your peripheral vision. When you turn your full gaze upon it, it vanishes and you doubt that it ever existed. Even this is consistent with scientific theory. Heisenberg's Uncertainty Principle, taught in any high school chemistry or physics class, shows that to know one thing about an electron, its position, is to preclude knowing another thing, its momentum."

Max continued: "Einstein said 'To know that what is impenetrable to us really exists, manifesting itself as the highest wisdom and most radiant beauty which our dull faculties can comprehend only in their most primitive forms — this knowledge, this feeling, is at the center of true religiousness. In this sense, and in this sense only, I belong to the ranks of devoutly religious men.' And Einstein was not only a devoutly religious man in that sense, but he was also the high priest of a religion we call physics. You do understand that Einstein derived his Theory of Relativity by having a shamanic vision, don't you? He dreamed up a hypothetical situation in which a clock and a candle were on a table and he rode the beam of light emanating from the flame. Then he asked himself the question 'What would I see if I looked back at the clock and the candle while riding away at the speed of light?' Out of his answer to that question came the basis for nuclear energy. And without him and the revelations that he brought forth, nothing I've done would be possible."

"Do we know the source of this energy?" I asked.

"You're missing the point," Max replied. "To be conscious, fully conscious, does not eliminate the mystery of life. That is why the most advanced quantum physicist still has honest room in his mind as well as his soul for a divinity. As a matter of fact, it's probable that every person we've ever associated with divinity was, in practice, a quantum physicist. They just didn't bother to get a degree." He paused. "It would have interfered with their productive years."

Ignoring my expression of pain at his joke, he continued:

"All energy comes from a higher source. All energy *is* the higher source. We don't create it, we just tap into it. You may call energy "divine," you may call it "eternal." They are synonyms. We are a church because we believe in energy and its eternal nature. The name you give to that energy is your choice, which we respect and encourage. We do not and cannot create it. That is the domain of the higher source. Call it God, Christ, Buddha, what you will. That part of it is out of our arena. We can simply use that energy given to you and help you direct it towards your well-being. We are not the source and we are not the object. Which, as I see it, is consistent with the teachings of any church. A church does not create life. It teaches you to tap in to the essence of life's creative force, which is, in and of itself, miraculous."

"Do you believe that energetic balancing work is miraculous?" I asked.

"Everything is miraculous," he replied. "The question is: Is it timely? Miracles appear for mankind when they are needed. The plagues of ignorance and unconsciousness are already here and I'm building the army to fight them. The solution, as in any war, is a combination of technology and manpower. This is where the training begins, and this is where we'll do the testing.

"People recognize their inner needs aren't being met, they're itching for change but they don't know how to get there. But people who have come here for energetic balancing find that their feelings of well-being return, they have drastically more energy, they think more clearly, their emotions are calmer, more centered, more loving. Remember the old adage about the Buddha getting a toothache? If the Buddha gets a toothache, there is no enlightenment, there is only the toothache."

"Where did that come from?" I asked him.

"Actually, I made it up," he replied. "But do you deny it?"

He turned back to the computer and clicked keys until a screen I had never seen before came up. He grabbed my thumb.

"I've been working on something new," he said. "Something that, again, was part of the promise of the initial vision, but it took a long time to make it precise."

What he had on the screen, according to its label, was the frequency for measurement of an individual's life force. He began testing me, running through a series of screens designed to come up with a number on a scale of one to a hundred. I came up in the mid-nineties.

"That's pretty good," he said.

I asked him what a bad reading was.

"Typically, I can't help anyone whose life force has ebbed below a certain number," he said. "It renders their energetic imbalance irreversible."

I thought about my own life-force reading. "Has anybody got a hundred?"

"Not so far."

"Why not?" I wondered. "Why don't I have a hundred, for instance?"

"This life force is spiritual force," he said. "The factors that affect it aren't just gross vibrations."

"What else?" I was starting to develop an intense personal interest in what might be keeping me from a perfect score.

Max laughed, recognizing my interest for what it was. He ran through a set of screens for emotional and psychological imbalances, came up with some issues for me.

"My sense is that these aren't what we're looking for," he said, clicking on to another screen titled "Spiritual Imbalances."

He ran through test after test, finally coming up with "Unresolved past life disappointment." I was stunned.

"What am I supposed to do with that?" I asked. "Unresolved past life disappointment? How do I resolve it?"

"What caused it?" Max asked. "Maybe in that past life you were a woodpecker and encountered an iron pole."

I grimaced. He shrugged.

"Who knows? In any case, we don't resolve it by giving you a two-by-four so you can do it right this time. Remember, the thing I am finding is a frequency, an energetic imbalance in you. We deal with it the same way we deal with all energetic imbalances: We find its frequency and find what frequency will remove it."

Instantly, he had put the discussion of something that seemed alien back onto familiar turf.

"The cause of an imbalance may be absurd, trivial, even moronic. It's the effect that matters," he elaborated. "And the effect is a negative energetic field. Remove that negative energy and your way of dealing with life will no longer be filtered through that negativity. And it doesn't matter whether you still can or cannot peck a good hole in a tree, does it? Maybe you were a virus and you weren't good at killing anyone and that's why you're bitter. What are you going to do about it?

"It doesn't matter what made you bitter. What matters is the negative energy that you're carrying with you now. Above and beyond that what matters is what you have to do to remove that energetic field. It certainly doesn't matter if you learn to dig a better hole in a proper tree with your beak, does it? Because you're not a woodpecker now, are you? Maybe you will be in your next life, but not now. So we resolve the problems the same way we find them: In energetic terms.

"That's why Wilhelm Reich departed from Freud. He thought it was unnecessary to try to relive a negative experience. He felt one could transcend it by removing the energetic block it created. The memory is not the issue. It's the impact it has. What kind of incident does it take to hurt someone or screw them up? It can be nothing. It can even be an imperception on their part. Nothing negative was done to you but the negative energy was there anyway. And even if the original victims are dead, the negative energy persists in *you*. There are untold millions, maybe billions, of people who are crippled by the effects of unresolved conflicts which are no longer relevant."

I thought about what Max was saying. I pointed out that, in my opinion, he was walking the blurry line between psychology and spirituality.

"That's because you insist on separating the body, the mind and the spirit," Max answered. "Despite the fact that your life's work is to unify them."

"With what?" I asked.

"Energy," Max said. "You keep using terms that are inappropriate. Remember, we don't practice medicine and we don't do therapy. We do energetic balancing."

"I know that," I answered.

"Yes, but you don't know why. And that's why you ask the wrong questions and make the wrong distinctions. Ask yourself what the difference is between vibration, energy and prayer or chanting."

I shrugged.

"It's all the same thing," he said. "It's a focusing of consciousness. The Lost Book of Confucius supposedly contained specific mantras for all the ills of mankind, but it is, as the name implies, lost. We have before us, in this machine, the new incarnation of that Lost Book. And what we do, once we identify the correct mantra for you, is put the mantra directly into your photograph. You don't have to chant it yourself.

"We are like the priests in the temples in Tibet, who for a fee will spin a prayer wheel for you. Our distinction is that we construct a personalized prayer wheel. We ask you, your higher self, that part of you which is completely conscious, to tell us exactly what prayer you need. Then we pray for you by spinning your personal energetic prayer wheel.

"We believe that creating this energetic mantra, this prayer wheel, has healing benefits. And no one can dispute the possibility of prayer or mantras or chanting as having healing benefits. But the fact that we use the healing power of prayer, rather than medicine, is why we're a church, not a hospital.

"There are people who are not physicians and yet *they* are called healers, and people with maladies seek them out in the hope that some higher consciousness in these healers will enable them overcome their maladies. What *we* do is help you find *your* higher consciousness, which we believe is resident in everyone, so that you become your own healer.

"No one can say it's absurd to believe in the healing power of prayer and no one can demand you get a prescription for a prayer — yours or, for that matter, ours."

The Choir

OVER THE NEXT few days, I settled in to life at Sanctuary. I saw Terry a few times. She was spending her time looking after Jane, who was feeling somewhat stronger, which allowed her to complain more vigorously. As it turned out there were quite a few people staying at Sanctuary, in the cabins strewn about in the hillsides. I asked Max what they were all doing there.

"I think it's time for you to meet the choir," he said.

"The choir?" I asked.

"That's what I call them," he said, "because I keep preaching to them. But they prefer to think of themselves as the apostles."

So I followed him back down to the hall again. This time there was a dozen people bustling inside, half with their thumbs out and the other half doing energetic evaluation. The room was a cacophony of squeals from the six computers in use.

"Meet the boys," said Max. He turned to them. "I brought you a new thumb."

"Thank God," said one of the most attractive of the "boys," a woman in her mid-thirties. She jumped up and began massaging her hand. "He can take my place."

I looked her over carefully and said, "It's a big chair. Why don't we share?"

She flashed a smile but, unfortunately, I found myself alone in the chair. The tester was an equally attractive woman.

"Hi, I'm Pamela," she said. "Let's test your aura."

She selected the appropriate menu and began the familiar process. All the tones were high-pitched. She came up with nothing in her screening.

"What does that mean?" Max asked her.

"He doesn't have an aura?" she guessed. "I think you brought in a ringer."

"Try turning down the current," Max said.

Slightly embarrassed, Pamela did so and began the process again. This time there was a positive. Looking at the screen, I saw she was checking the color of my inner aura.

"Blue," Pamela said. "Self-reliance. I like that in a man."

She went on to check my middle aura.

"Bright blue. Confidence," she said.

I preened, in full control of the situation.

My outer aura came up green, for adaptability. She set up for another test — the spiritual aura. It came up violet for intuition.

"I think she's going to be a great tester," I said to Max.

"There's one more aura feature to check," Pamela said, fishing around on the screen. "Auric overlay."

She abused my thumb some more and came up with deep scarlet. The associated emotional feature was lust.

"What are you doing tonight?" I asked her.

Ignoring me, she checked my ideal aura — golden, for higher thought. "Most people show golden as their ideal," she said.

"And?" I said.

"And the answer to your question about tonight is that I wouldn't dream of interfering with your ideal."

"Check him for damage to the aura," Max instructed her.

She set the machine up for another run and it indicated positive. Checking for its cause, she came up with the frequency of chemical toxicity. She checked further.

"It's MSG," she said.

"Easy to get rid of," Max said.

"Great," I replied. I turned back to Pamela. "You want to go out for Chinese food?"

Over the next few days, my thumb was at the disposal of the choir. Pamela turned out to be a practicing clinical psychologist with a predilection for finding energetic imbalances relating to emotion in the subtle energetic bodies. Fortunately, Max had many pictures of volunteers, including the apostles and other denizens of Sanctuary.

In my next session as Pamela's thumb, we were evaluating Terry's picture for negative emotions. The dominant negative emotions was "inflexibility," a quality I'd observed more than once in Terry.

Pamela said, "Let's see why."

She then began to check Terry's photo, layer by energetic layer. The first thing we found was a frequency identified with deficiency of a hormone, oxytocin.

Max, watching, said, "We keep asking our only question until there are no more answers."

Pamela nodded, but I asked Max just what that question was.

"Why," he replied.

"Because I'm interested," I told him.

"No," he laughed. "Remember Abbot and Costello's 'Who's on First?' The question we're asking is 'why?'"

Pamela tested and said, "On the surface it's caused by the frequency of aluminum toxicity."

"I thought aluminum was a rather flexible metal," I wisecracked.

"Under that," Pamela continued tersely, applying the probe to my thumb with greater vehemence, "we find the frequency of a psychoneuroimmunological imbalance."

"Where does it begin?" Max asked.

She checked and answered, "At the emotional level." She pressed my thumb again. "Self pity... caused by... a color imbalance."

"A color imbalance?" This reminded me of the aura testing we had done earlier.

"Caused by..." She hesitated, looked at Max. "A viral frequency that's not in the database, Max."

"It's time for me to take over," he answered. He got the attention of the others. "All of you, I want you to watch this, and take notes."

He began to fly from screen to screen and actually in front of us figured out the exact frequency of Terry's unknown virus frequency, using her picture and my thumb.

"So this is an unknown virus?" I asked.

"*Was* unknown," Max said. "No one's going to remember a number, so in the future this frequency will be in the database as TFV1 for Terry Fisher Virus number one. Okay, Pamela, now you tell us *where* she has it."

Pamela took the probe again and after a few moments answered, "The frequency is in the spinal medulla... cervical... thoracic... lumbar and sacral."

Max said, "It's everywhere in her spine. Does that sound like an inbalance that might cause inflexibility?" He turned to Pamela. "How long has she had this frequency?"

Pamela paged to the appropriate tray. "More than days... weeks... she's had it for months.. eight months."

"Then she picked it up since the last time she came in to see me," Max said. "She hadn't been in the office for almost a year." He laughed. "It was a frequency with her name on it. It'll be gone in a week."

One day I played thumb for another apostle, bearded like in the old days, who introduced himself as Doug. That day I got to be a movie star, though unfortunately the wrong sex, because our first photographic subject was a face easily recognized by me and probably most of the rest of the planet, by virtue of all her movies and television series. She was a friend of Jennifer's and had agreed to have her initial evaluation be used as a training session for new testers. In the public perception, she was a perfect and virtually flawless woman. But that was not going to be the case revealed by our energetic analysis.

"Does she have any problems she wants addressed?" Doug asked Max.

"Yes," Max said, "as a matter of fact she does. She's dyslexic and as a matter of fact so is her son, which should give you some kind of a hint, Doug."

"I've got it," Doug said. "It runs in the family."

"I knew your medical training would come in handy," Max answered.

Max turned to me and said, "Doug is actually Dr. Douglas Richards. He is something of an expert on other vibrational healing techniques and found himself interested in the work we do."

"More than interested," Doug said. "I've been tested and nuked and certified clean."

"Nuked?" I asked.

"That's what I call it when Max pumps energy into my picture," he laughed.

"Technically, the correct term is 'frying,'" Jennifer piped in, as she slipped a few more pictures onto imprinting plates nearby.

Doug began testing, initially looking for hereditary imbalances.

"Look at this," he said, "the frequency of hereditary encephalitis."

Max looked at Jennifer and said, "That accounts for her blonde hair."

"What accounts for your celibacy?" Jennifer replied, sweetly.

"Truce?" Max asked.

"Accepted. For the moment." Jennifer turned back to her computer.

Doug looked at Max. "Encephalitis is supposed to be a rare disease," he said, "but we've been finding its energetic signature quite commonly. It certainly is consistent with her dyslexia problem."

"See if you can find an energetic cause for her dyslexia when you're done with the primary evaluation," Max said.

Doug continued his testing. "Here's one she shouldn't have to concern herself with. She's got a hereditary nose cold, the frequency of a rhinovirus."

"As a matter of fact," Jennifer said, "she's always complaining about how nasal her voice sounds."

Doug continued testing. And in each case, Jennifer commented on the relationship between our energetic findings and a problem in our subject:

"Oh, there's her constipation," and "That's why she's always scratching," and "No wonder her teeth are crooked," and so on.

Soon Doug finished testing for hereditary imbalances and began looking for active imbalances.

"Look at that!" said Doug. "Another encephalitis frequency — this time it's active."

"See how long she's had it," Max directed.

Doug probed and said, "Twenty-eight years."

"That would mean she was four years old when she got it," Jennifer said.

"Remember this," Max said. "If you have measles and you get a rash, that's normal. It's not worthy of contemplation. But if you continue to get rashes over time, you'd have to be a moron not to ask why. It's obvious: You get a cold, so you sneeze. That wouldn't account for your sneezing for five straight years. There's no such thing as not getting rid of a cold unless, of course, you have no immune system. There's no such thing as anything without a reason. And if you can't find a reason, it means *you can't find it,* not that there is none. We have to remember we are not the *raison d'etre*, not the bottom line. We're simply investigators. Our blindness or stupidity isn't a conclusion. Our failure to comprehend or perceive something isn't proof that it doesn't exist. To primitive organisms, ignorance may be bliss. For us, it's frustration, a challenge and a command to dig in our heels and try again. We transcend the ecstacy of ignorance. And I've got to warn you," Max laughed, "if you join me, you'll lose that source of mindless pleasure. You'll know that what you don't know *can* and *does* hurt you. Innocence is for children; as a child you're entitled to its protection. As an adult, however, innocence becomes ignorance, which does not exist in a state of grace and offers no protection from anything. That is why our priests will not be cloistered monks, protected from the ways of the world. They will have to know more about the energetic imbalances of life than those they are trying to help. Otherwise, they'll be useless. Our path to consciousness is found in life, not in death, not in the hereafter.

"What it boils down to is this," he finished. "Long-term energetic problems *always* have a hereditary base coupled with the active imbalance. I call it the energetic template. We'll soon see if it applies to her."

"I see she's got the frequency of a respiratory flu," Doug said. "I wonder if she has the frequency of a cough."

"Leave the jokes to me," Max said.

"I thought the tester got the punchlines," Doug protested.

Max grudgingly acquiesced.

Continuing, Doug found frequencies for a couple of skin problems, arthritis and, as usual, TB, which caused him to comment, "We're finding this in everybody."

"Doug, you're an MD," Max said. "By your collective standard, it's simple and you know how it works: If a doctor tests you for TB and you test positive, you probably have it. On the other hand, if the test is negative, you simply have what you doctors call idiopathic night sweats, dry cough and unilateral shoulder and back pains. I can't address the biological presence of TB. All I know is that when we remove the *frequency* of TB, my clients report that a lot of their complaints disappear."

"What do you tell them?" Doug asked.

"I tell them it's a coincidence," Max replied. "While you're working with the church, Doug, you're never going to diagnose TB or any other disease. While you and I may both help people, I don't do it by treating disease. I do it by removing negative energetic frequencies."

Doug nodded.

"Now let's see how much of this ties in to the cause of the frequency of her dyslexia," Max said.

Doug set up the machine to look for the energetic basis of the dyslexia frequency. He resumed testing and said, "The most external cause is the frequency of heavy metal toxicity."

"Aluminum?" I asked.

He tested again. "Nope. Mercury. In her brain."

"Another shiny metal," Max frowned. "All things considered, luster is not a desirable quality in a brain."

"Under that," said Doug, continuing the evaluation, "we have the active encephalitis resonance. That makes sense. And here's the hereditary encephalitis."

"Anything else?" Max asked.

Doug ran through the rest of the screens. "That's all," he concluded.

"One last question," said Max. "Is there any frequency we can use that will negate the frequency of dyslexia?"

Doug checked and said, "There is one. A gem elixir. Moonstone." He went on to find a specific energetic potency that would be most effective.

"Excellent," Max said. "At that potency, it's no longer molecular, so we can either give her the actual remedy or simply imprint its frequency into her picture. It makes it real convenient."

Jane's First Re-evaluation

THE SETTING was the same as the last time, Max holding the probe, the rest of us looking at the monitor. Jane was the only salient difference. Today, she was alert, animated and radiating an air of positivism, rather than her previous fatalism.

"Let's see how you're doing," said Max. He began testing.

He immediately went to the malignancy frequency he had found before, and again it was positive.

"I hoped it would be gone." Jane visibly sagged. "I feel like it's going."

"I told you it would take about a month," Max answered. "It's only been two weeks."

He pressed some buttons and tested her again. He wasn't satisfied with the result, so he hit another button, tested again. A few more repetitions provided the answer he was looking for.

He pointed at the screen. "This number represents the current strength of this particular malignancy frequency," he told her. "When you started, the number indicated that the frequency was powerful and active, whereas now it's barely there and it's having no negative effect on you."

"Will it ever be gone?" Jane asked.

Max said, "Right now, it's about one minute closer to being gone than it was the last time you asked that question."

"So I won't have cancer in two weeks?" Jane persisted.

"You won't have the *frequency* of cancer," he said.

"What about the cancer?"

"You'll have to see your MD to determine that," he told her.

He began testing again. Referring to his notes from her initial evaluation, Max revisited each frequency he had found, testing for presence and current strength.

He looked at her and said, "You're improving as rapidly as is possible. All these frequencies will be gone." He tested again. "Your life force is at the moron level."

She looked at the screen, scowling.

"That's good news," Max laughed. "Last time, you were an imbecile. Measuring life force against the IQ scale, that is. But don't feel bad: since we're only measuring on a scale of one to a hundred, there aren't any life force geniuses."

Jane's face was blank. She wasn't following him.

Max patted her hand. "I'm teasing you," he said. He picked up the probe again. "Let's see what other frequencies show."

He resumed testing, going through the entire sequence of a full energetic analysis. He came up with several other frequencies.

"Good news," he told her. "You've got the frequency of a cold."

"What's so good about that?" Jane sniffled.

"Because when your malignancy frequency was strong enough, it wouldn't let anything that innocuous inside. In other words, the malignancy frequency is losing its dominance over you."

Jane's smile reflected her understanding that her long ordeal was coming to a close.

"Terry told me about the emotional evaluation," she said. "Can we do that now?"

"Nope," Max answered. "You can't have everything first. You've got to get past this level before you deal with anything else. I'm afraid you're still stuck with two weeks."

He put down the probe.

Doug's Ideas

THAT NIGHT after dinner I had a chance to question Doug about his opinion as both an MD and, according to Max, an expert theorist in matters vibrational. I cornered him in the great room of the hacienda where he was reading and enjoying a glass of wine. At first, Doug modestly disclaimed any special knowledge, but soon he waxed philosophical about the implications and capabilities of subtle energy analysis.

"As an MD, I always felt that I was only working with a small part of the equation," he admitted. "I believe the roots of well-being go much deeper and to a much more fundamental place than the biological concept of 'absence of disease' which is currently the standard used by medical practitioners. Current scientific thinking doesn't take the full complexity of our being-ness into account. We've been reduced to meat machines, not the magnificent multidimensional entities that we really are."

I expressed surprise at his attitude and he smiled.

"Earning an MD isn't necessarily the equivalent of an academic lobotomy," he said. "Like many other people, I've always known that I am more than a body, and I've kept that knowledge throughout my professional training."

"What do you mean by 'more than a body?'" I asked.

"You know what I mean," he chided. "Max told me you've been working with him for a long time." He looked at me like I was trying to pull something over on him.

I replied that I especially wanted to hear his interpretation.

He thought for a moment or two.

"There is a new view of the body emerging," he reflected. "It sees it as something more than a mere biomechanism. This energetic viewpoint is based on new discoveries in science about the basic nature of the matter which makes up our bodies and the world around us. At the subatomic level, all matter, including the molecules that make up the human body, is actually a form of frozen, vibrating energy. As such, one can view the body not only as a biomechanism, but also as a kind of unique, vibrating energy system.

"Of course, you already know that the body is regulated by control systems. Some of these use molecular signals, such as hormones, but others use energetic signals, like the electrical pulses in the nerves, to transmit information and help the body maintain a state of balance and health."

Doug paused. "This is the surprising thing," he continued. "Medical researchers working on bone fractures which were having problems mending discovered that they could send an electromagnetic signal to the fracture to stimulate rapid healing. It seems that the electromagnetic frequency was carrying the same message as a chemical produced by the cells of the body."

I wasn't sure what Doug was getting at.

"I believe," he said, "that for *every* chemical or molecular signal that the body uses, there may be an equivalent electromagnetic frequency that will transmit the same message."

"Is electromagnetism the same thing as subtle energy?" I asked.

"Actually, no," Doug confessed. "But for every chemical, molecular or electromagnetic signal, there seems to be a corresponding subtle-energy frequency as well."

"I see," I said. "So Max's energetic balancing reinforces the body's internal regulatory system."

"It goes beyond that," he said. "In fact, that would be a highly simplified view. There are some other factors that we have to consider to get a more complete picture of the possibilities. Do you know much about holograms?"

I knew that holograms were three-dimensional pictures, I told him. And supposedly any piece of a hologram contains the entire hologram.

"That's true," he said, "but remember that you have to use a laser as the light source in order to see the entire hologram in each piece of the hologram."

"So how does this relate to what Max does?" I asked.

"The holographic principle appears to apply to the human body as well. On one level, we know that every cell of the body contains the same master DNA library of genes as every other cell of the body."

"That's why they could clone a sheep, for instance," I volunteered.

"Exactly," he said. "DNA, as a chemical construct, illustrates one aspect of the holographic principle applied to the body. If you look at the human body as a unique energetic system, like a physicist would, where it's made up of various frequencies of energy held in place as the atoms and molecules of the body's tissues, then theoretically the body also energetically contains all the information of the whole coded in an energetic form as well. Certain researchers in Europe and in the United States have found that they can decode the biological frequency information of the human body from specimens of hair or blood taken from someone, or even by utilizing photographs of the individual."

"I presume this is leading somewhere?" I still wasn't sure where he was going with this information.

"Absolutely," he said. "You asked me for my interpretation. Are you presuming that this information is so simple that it can be delivered in a single sentence?"

"Of course not," I replied sheepishly.

"This is one of the interesting dilemmas in talking about this material," he said. "Because most people are used to talking about the world in a certain way, a way which is rooted in the scientific dogma of the early part of this century. In other words, common wisdom, which is often an oxymoron anyway, is based on information that is almost a hundred years old and in the case of Isaac Newton, several hundred years old. For us to talk about Max's work, we have to base some of our conversation on work that is more recent."

"So this is a complete departure from anything else in history?" I asked.

"You must have read my mind.," he said. "I was just about to bring up an example that addresses that question. Actually, some of the basis of energetic balancing goes back thousands of years. According to the theories of ancient Chinese acupuncture, the body contains pathways for life force energy. They call the pathways 'meridians.' Finally, western science has validated the existence of these energy pathways by injecting radioactive tracers into acupuncture points and then following the radioactive material down the meridians. More elegant methods use special electrical probes which are connected to sensitive testing equipment which measures the electrical energy of these meridians when you touch them to the acupuncture points."

"That sounds like what Max does," I commented.

"It is a part of what Max does on the surface," he replied. "But Max has gone far beyond what anyone else is able to do. Do you know about homeopathy?"

"Like cures like," I said, echoing the basic principle of that philosophy. "I call it 'hair of the dog that bit you' treatment."

He smiled. "Homeopaths figured out that extremely-weak tinctures contained the energetic information of the original substances, even though the chemical information was gone. Interestingly, the more dilution there was, the

stronger the energetic qualities were, almost as if the physical qualities interfered with the energetic qualities. These
energetic remedies have been used to assist the body in
healing and rebalancing. More recently, it has been discovered that we don't need the original plant substances. The
pure energetic frequencies alone can be sent to the body to
bring about rebalancing."

"Who discovered that?" I wondered.

"Max," he replied.

"It still sounds like we're talking about the body," I said.
"You started by saying that you believe that we're more
than just our bodies."

"We are energetic systems," he declared. "If you include
that in your definition of the body, then we're on the same
wavelength. But that is not a definition of the body that I
would agree with if you asked my opinion as an MD."

"And your opinion as a person?" I prompted.

"You're implying that doctors aren't people," he chided,
grinning.

I looked at him guilelessly and he continued.

"My opinion is that we are complex energetic systems
and we can derive great improvements in our well-being by
using Max's energetic balancing. He is able to examine our
total being, physical, mental, emotional and spiritual, in
terms of pure subtle-energy frequencies. Max is able to obtain this energetic information directly from the body by
measuring the energetic status of acupuncture points on the
skin, as well as by using a photographic image of the individual being tested. He can detect problem areas of imbal-

ance and provide the body with the correct rebalancing frequencies in several different ways, one of which is to transfer the energy into a bottle of liquid which can then be
taken as drops under the tongue, and another is to transfer
the energy directly into the person's picture. Which brings
us back to that idea of the hologram: It is as if, at least for
energetic purposes, the individual is a hologram and the
photograph is a piece of that hologram, thus we can both
measure and change a person's energetic status using their
photograph."

"And the machine Max uses is the laser, the coherent
light source, that lets you see the piece the same as you
would see the whole?" I asked.

Doug smiled, nodded, then: "On one level, I think
what Max is doing is a development of 21st century science."

"What's the other level?" I asked.

He looked at me, serious and quiet. "The other level is
something more amazing than a major scientific advance."

I waited.

"The more I've learned from doing the testing," he said,
"the more I think that Max is truly working with the spirit-
essence, if you know what I mean."

"I think I do," I said.

"My name for what he does is 'energetic repatterning' or
'spiritual repatterning,' not for any reason other than that
I'm still trying to fully grasp it and a new name seems to
make me feel better. And I think he's erasing old karmic
patterns. Karma, in the eastern view, is intrinsically bad be-

cause it ties the spirit to old habits, old fates, which are repeated until some lesson is learned. The work Max does releases these things very quickly. Starting with gross imbalances and working through subtler and subtler energetic layers, he works with the body, mind and spirit, clearing out old baggage. The end result is an individual who is free to make choices because he or she is no longer carrying the burden of the past."

Somewhere during this talk, Terry came over and sat down next to me, listening quietly to Doug talk.

"Are you talking about past lives?" she asked, interjecting for the first time.

He nodded. "Reincarnation and past life trauma are part of what's emerging in this system. Max's vibrational work has transcended the physical, which is now merely the prerequisite for doing truly deep-level subtle energetic work which involves contact with the higher or causal self." He paused, looking over my shoulder.

I turned. Max had joined us.

"Imbalances emerge when we cut ourselves off from the higher self, which is our true self," Max said. "When we are cut off, we act against our own higher instincts, interests and motivations, which are largely altruistic and service-oriented. These things relate to our life-tasks, the reasons we chose to have bodies and be in this place. We already have knowledge of all of our past lives and what we need to do for further growth now. The trick is to remember what we already know."

"Now I'm lost a little," I said. "How does this life-purpose and higher self stuff relate to what vibrational balancing or energetic repatterning or whatever you want to call it?"

Doug deferred again to Max.

"We are energetic beings," Max said simply. "We are ebbs and flows of life-force energies. The more freely the life-force flows in us, the better we are able to perform the tasks we came here to perform. The impediments to that flow are also energetic. We now know they can be detected and erased, layer by energetic layer."

He turned to Doug. "Have you told them about the work you and I have been doing?"

Doug shook his head. "Not without your consent."

"I consent," Max said, then excused himself to join Jennifer.

"Are you aware of the subtle-energy functions of what medicine calls the 'glands' or 'endocrine system?'" Doug asked us.

Terry and I both shook our heads.

"This is an interesting illustration of what I've been saying," he continued. "Each gland, according to energetic traditions dating back thousands of years, has functions that relate to integration of the self with the higher self. Did you know that medical research has shown that people who meditate achieve drastically higher physiological function in the glandular system?"

Again, we shook our heads.

"Ultimately, there is a progression of energetic cleansing that works through the subtle body we all possess, and activates each of the glands until finally the pineal gland, the seat of the spirit, opens and we achieve complete communion with our higher selves."

Terry and I sat silently, absorbing everything he had said.

He shrugged. "You wanted my interpretation," he said.

The Thumb Chronicles
Part I

DURING THE COURSE of the next few weeks, I spent the greater part of each day being... a *thumb*, which, of course, became increasingly frustrating. Other "thumbs" were provided by testers-in-training, who practiced on each other with photographs of Max's choosing, so he would always know what they should be finding in each one. I rotated among them, and among the newly-certified testers who had already climbed through Max's hierarchy of expertise to the point where they were ready to test the ever-expanding stack of photographs from new Sanctuary members. But I stayed on the same side of the desk.

Each time I asked Max to begin training me to test, his reply was the same: "Not yet." When pressed, he'd elaborate, "I need you to observe more. And take notes on what we're finding."

And so, to my chagrin, I had the dual jobs of recording secretary and permanent thumb. Max took me off duty with the trainees and had me work only with him or the testers who had passed the training phase.

To my surprise, over time I began to see patterns emerge in the people who were being tested. In one sense, the patterns were general and I began to see what Max meant by "the plague." We checked people all over the planet. At times, we would check people from the same area and see the same things occurring. When that happened, Max had the tester check for an energetic "epidemic factor" in that area.

*   *   *

Frighteningly, an enormous number of people showed the frequency of HIV and, in almost every case, it showed the frequency of "airborne transmission." And in each case, Max had the tester examine the consequences, which varied from person to person, though within a range which quickly became predictable: All had frequencies indicating the same immune deficiency factors; in fact, they were the same as those showing for the people who had acquired the frequency of HIV through more conventional means.

This first revelation, about the ubiquity of HIV and a number of other frequencies which indicated life-threatening immune deficiencies, was a shock to me.

"Do you think the people we've been testing are a representative sample?" I asked Max, worried about the implications of how widespread the frequency of the disease might be.

"If so, at this rate, within five years this frequency will show in more than half the country... and probably more than half the world," he replied, somberly. "But the good news is that, like everything else I find, we're talking about an energetic imbalance. And energetic imbalances are totally erasable."

Oddly, we would find these frequencies repeatedly in many people. After the frequency had been erased, they would often acquire it again via what tested out to be airborne sources. But, over time, they began developing resistance to the frequency and further testing indicated that for these people the frequency of HIV was self-limiting and would go away on its own.

"This fits the way people acquire resistance to any plague," Max said. "When the Black Death spread through medieval Europe, the population immediately lived out the old adage 'That which does not kill you makes you stronger.' Which of course is no consolation to the dead..."

I was struck, suddenly, by remembering what I had read of the way bubonic plague ran its course in those long ago times. "Didn't the plague last sixty to eighty years?" I asked Max.

He nodded. "It took almost fifteen years for them to recognize that it *was* a plague."

"Why did it end?" I asked.

"It obviously wasn't a gesture of consideration by the fleas or the rats," Max said. "It took that long to develop a population of survivors with immunity."

"What would happen to this person without energetic intervention?" I asked Max, tapping the photo which lay face-down on the sample tray.

"Let's look." Max ran through some more screens, first ascertaining a projected life span without the appropriate balancing frequencies.

It was three years.

The answer *with* energetic intervention was eighty-nine years.

I was stunned. "Does this person have any symptoms now?" I asked.

Max turned to the Request for Balancing sheet in which the person listed her problems. "Crushing headache, nausea, fatigue, fits of rage." He tossed the paper aside. "These are the usual complaints with the onset of this frequency."

I was surprised when Max turned the picture over to show it to me, because he was normally meticulous about guarding the privacy, confidentiality and identity of his clients. It was Jennifer's daughter.

"Amy's only eleven years old," he said. "Don't worry, she'll be better than perfect in a couple of days."

"Better?" I asked.

"She's developing an immunity," he told me. "She'll be the next generation. It only comes from exposure, you know. Not from thinking good thoughts or being a vegetarian. Immunity comes from exposure — *if* you survive."

*   *   *

The energetic signature of cancer was routinely found in the pictures we were evaluating. Shockingly, the people who had them were often in their twenties and thirties. Max pointed out a series of energetic environmental factors that invariably showed up in their pictures. These environmental factors had emerged quite recently and were apparently causing a very high incidence of cancer frequencies.

"That is," he added, "assuming these frequencies have any relationship to what we think of as the physical world. Or, more importantly, what *they* think of as the physical world."

Once, looking over some of the Request For Evaluation forms, I noted that most of the people in whom we had found the frequency of cancer that day didn't indicate a medical diagnosis of cancer among their complaints.

"Does this mean their cancer isn't yet very advanced?" I asked Max.

"Remember," he said, "that we are finding frequencies. We are not finding cancer, that's not what we do."

"We usually find the frequency of cancer in those who come to us with medically diagnosed cancer," I pointed out.

"It's an interesting correlation, isn't it?" he replied. "But we don't diagnose or cure disease. Luckily, we are usually able to identify and remove energetic imbalances."

Sometimes the work was scary, especially when we found cancer frequencies. Some of those who had them couldn't pass the Eligibility Evaluation. Max had designed this evaluation to ensure that people who came to Sanctuary, either in person or photographically, were able to

benefit from energetic balancing. Some of the factors ana-
lyzed whether the person had an innate or constitutional
inability to benefit from energetic testing. Though that
condition was relatively rare, it did appear at times. More
commonly, and more tragically, we sometimes found that
people who were very sick or very weak no longer had
enough life-force energy to benefit from energetic balancing.

One person we turned away had been medically diagnosed with pancreatic cancer. In the Request For Evaluation, he had indicated that the cancer was spreading rapidly
and was inoperable. Unfortunately, the Eligibility Evaluation indicated that Max could do nothing for him energetically. We heard a few weeks later that he died.

Going through the records we were keeping, I pointed
out a similar situation to Max. Another person we had
evaluated had a medically-diagnosed pancreatic cancer, was
also diagnosed to be inoperable, but had passed the Eligibility Evaluation. After being energetically balanced several
times, the person had reported that they were feeling great
and had written to tell Max that their doctors had diagnosed
him cancer-free, attributing the miraculous recovery to
spontaneous remission.

"Haven't you noticed that two people can be exposed to
the same disease?" he asked. "One becomes violently ill and
dies. The other feels a little off for a few days and is then
fine. There are numerous cases of identical twins, one of
whom gets a dread disease and the other doesn't. And yet
their pattern of exposure appears to be identical. The dif-

ference is in the ability or inability of one or the other to resist. That is what energetic balance and imbalance is about. The difference isn't the disease, it's the energetic balance of the individuals involved. The disease we leave to doctors. Whether the disease is the common cold, pimples, emotional upset or cancer, we don't deal with it. We deal with the energetic balance of the individual."

After a moment's reflection, he continued: "This becomes an illustration of what we mean when we say that we don't deal with disease. It's a given that a lot of germs are ubiquitous. Yet some people get sick, others don't. Some people have the energetic balance that allows them to deal with the disease effectively; others don't. But whether they do or do not have these diseases isn't relevant to our testing. If they have a given frequency, we remove the frequency and hope that their bodies will then be interested in removing the pathogen. That is why we have no interest in lab tests — we don't work with diseases. We're only interested in the energetic balance of our clients."

✳   ✳   ✳

One of the most common problems listed in the Requests for Evaluation were "brain fog" or "air-headed" or "space cadet." Sometimes people would describe getting lost on the way home from work... if they remembered how to start their car. One woman tried to back out of her garage — without opening the door. She called in her request for evaluation from her cellular phone, sitting amidst the wreckage in her convertible, while her husband screamed at her in the background. Yet another, a prominent therapist, got in her new car, took the cap off her fruit drink and shook it violently to mix it up. She, too, was in tears. Over and over again, people complained "I'm turning into an idiot" or "I think I've caught Alzheimer's." In almost every case, the problem was the frequency of some kind of encephalitis. Western Equine, St. Louis, Venezuelan. Japanese. Russian.

"Aren't these supposed to be rare diseases?" I asked.

Doug, the MD, laughed and said, "There were three reported cases in Illinois last year — of which I personally had fourteen, if having the frequency counts. All from insect bites. If it wasn't for Max, I'd get rid of my dog and cat. I'd wake up, see them scratching and try to remember where the kitchen was, so I could make coffee."

I flashed back to the first time I had seen the frequency of encephalitis appear on Max's computer. I had been to the Los Angeles County Museum of Art and strolled by the La Brea Tar Pits. Oddly, there were signs posted to the fences warning passers-by to avoid the local mosquitos which were vectors of encephalitis. I pointed it out to my then-girlfriend, who had accompanied me to the museum. The next morning, she awoke with an excruciating headache. Her neck was so stiff she couldn't even turn her head. She was nearly paralyzed and unable to talk. I carried her to the car and took her to Max, who promptly found the frequency of Venezuelan Equine Encephalitis. Within two hours she was fully recovered.

I had asked Max how we were supposed to avoid the mosquitos.

"Duck?" he suggested.

*   *   *

Another pattern which emerged involved complaints of "tired, can't stay awake." One person reported that she had essentially stayed in bed for the past five years. In that case, the frequency was one that had no name and no corollary of a similar known disease, which of course didn't matter to Max. He found the frequency, named it after her, and it became part of the database. Amazingly, this frequency showed up regularly once it had been discovered and un-masked. In fact, one evening at Sanctuary I found myself unable to keep my eyes open in a conversation with Doug. After about a half an hour of trying to talk to me with my eyes closed and my mumbled responses, he excitedly dragged me down to the hall to test me. He quickly found the new frequency — in me. And once he began imprinting my photograph it took about twenty minutes for me to be up and about as if nothing had happened.

Doug said, "If you had had this a year ago, you could have had an energetic imbalance named after you. Now you'll have to be content with a library or a boat."

It looked like there had been a lot of competition trying to get that imbalance named after them. We got requests for evaluation from a race car driver who had fallen asleep at the wheel, hundreds of people who found themselves sleeping twelve to fifteen hours a day, people who figured their constant exhaustion and inability to keep their eyes open was a precursor of old age. If this last group had been correct, there were five-year-olds who were going on eighty-one.

But it wasn't the only frequency which caused exhaustion. There were many, in fact, all of which in some way undermined the energetic constitution of the person who had them. In every case, energetic balancing with the correct frequency resulted in the underlying imbalance disappearing. Subsequently, the tiredness would be replaced with renewed energy.

*   *   *

By far, the most common complaint involved a combination of night sweats, fever, dull cough, back pain which went up into one shoulder and... depression.

In fact, one woman called Max sobbing and said "I have TB."

"How do you know?" Max asked.

"I'm madly in love, my career is fantastic and I can't stop crying," she bawled.

"You're probably right," Max replied.

We tested her and she was on the money — she showed the frequency of two kinds of tuberculosis. She was obviously a veteran of Max's work.

"Every disease frequency has an associated emotion," Max explained. "With TB it's depression. Gonorrhea, on the other hand, causes wild and crazy behavior. Liver imbalances, like the frequency of hepatitis, cause anger... as in 'bilious.'"

But the frequency of TB was epidemic, pandemic, ubiquitous. Almost everybody had it. One strain was unique in that it caused a sugar craving. Another involved the lower back and genitourinary tract and stuffed ears. But no one seemed to be immune. Not even those with the frequency of cancer, which seemed to protect them against almost everything else, as we had seen with Jane. TB was, in fact, the frequency Max had found in me the first time I had been checked. Upon finding it, he had correctly described my chronic back pain and correctly predicted that it would go away in days. Over the ensuing years, the frequency became more and more commonly found in his energetic evaluations.

Out of curiosity, I did some research into the official position on the prevalence of TB. Checking newspaper and journal reports, I found that some articles indicated that it was a rare illness, while others indicated an incidence as high as eighty-five percent of the population. The incidence seemed to be highest among people testing positive for AIDS, so the conclusion was drawn that it was secondary to AIDS itself.

Max's response to my observation was to point out, "That's the group that's tested for TB the most. And the only group that's routinely 'cultured,' which is bound to skew the statistics."

He was referring to the use of a test in which doctors actually grew the TB bacteria in a sterile environment so they could identify the exact strain, as opposed to the skin test used most commonly. The culture test takes six to eight weeks to produce a result, thus it was both inconvenient and expensive, even though it was far more accurate than the skin test.

Max cautioned me. "The test indicates the actual disease. Remember, what we're finding is a frequency associated with a set of symptoms which obviously have no identifiable cause. This may or may not be TB, we don't know and can't know because the acceptable identifying tests are outside of our domain. We work with energy. Period."

As we worked, Max routinely had every tester, in response to the complaint of depression, check to see if it was "exogenous" or "endogenous." If it was the latter, the frequency of TB was almost always indicated as the causative factor.

As usual, imprinting the photographs of the people we tested produced the result that their complaints disappeared. There was almost as much incoming mail celebrating this as there was new pictures coming in with requests for evaluation.

Resolving the Unknowable

BY NOW, I had seen many hundreds of people evaluated photographically and seen their complaints correlated with energetic imbalances. Again and again, Max insisted that this work had nothing to do with disease or illness and everything to do with wellness. I constantly queried him about the relationship, though I remembered his detailed conversation with Jane. He patiently reiterated his position for me.

"Remember that we're never talking about disease in the orthodox sense of it, because the things we measure are not considered orthodox measures of disease. In the medical world, the presence of a disease is measured by proper identification of a disease organism, pathogen or antibody produced by the immune system as a defense against such an organism or pathogen. The techniques I use aren't acknowledged by any organized medical body in this country and in fact are not recognized as being relevant to modern allopathic medicine."

"We're been over this ground, Max. Aren't you splitting hairs?" I asked. "Isn't this a pretty fine distinction you're

drawing between your work and the work of medical doctors?"

He looked pained. "This is the how-many-angels-fit-on-
the-head-of-a-pin problem. On one level it's a fine point,
and on another level it's the *whole* point. *No medical authority recognizes this work as medicine or as medically valid or
medically relevant and I agree with them.* I do not detect disease. I detect disturbances in the subtle-energy field that is
your basic essence. Some people who have done research in
this area feel that there is a strong correlation between the
detection of certain frequencies and the presence of disease
organisms or pathogens. I say it's irrelevant, because information about the frequency of a subtle-energy disturbance is only good for removing that disturbance. I don't
do surgery. I don't use antibiotics. I don't do anything
medical or recommend anything medical. That isn't my
area of expertise. My area of expertise is in detecting and
correcting subtle-energy imbalances. Does this seem like
medicine to you?"

I had to admit that it didn't sound anything like medicine.

"Thank you," he nodded. "So to answer your question,
when we talk about the frequency of TB or the frequency of
HIV, we're not saying that TB or HIV is everywhere. I'm
simply saying that I often find frequencies that have been
associated with those problems. Interestingly enough, we
often find confirming information in the popular press or in
journals of epidemiology. Usually, people who manifest
these frequencies experience various rather-predictable de-
teriorations in their feeling of well-being. When their sub-

tle-energetic balance is restored, their feeling of well-being returns. I can't speak to whether or not they actually had TB, because I don't test for TB. If they want to know whether they have it, my clients go to an MD for the appropriate tests."

Max waited for some kind of response.

"But what about the coughing?" I asked.

"Coughing is a symptom of some kind of imbalance in the body," he replied. "Sometimes it means that you didn't swallow your own saliva correctly."

"So it doesn't mean somebody has TB?"

"Of course not. But I am convinced that even the subtlest discomforts are indicative of some kind of energetic imbalance. In homeopathy, they use a technique known as repertorizing, in which the homeopath encourages the patient to carefully examine their experiences about many aspects of their well-being. For the very best homeopaths, there are no irrelevant clues. In Sanctuary's energetic work, I also feel this is true. But it's important to make distinctions. I believe that each of us is a self-organizing energetic entity. We are constantly under attack from other energetic entities which seek to use our energies for themselves. On a macro level, you can think of examples like the food chain. On more micro levels, we might be talking about entropy, which is the loss of energy experienced by any energetic system, whether it be you, a tree, the solar system or the universe. You fight all these battles all the time. At the entropic level, you can look at your atomic structure and see it happening. The ability to overcome entropy is a key charac-

teristic of living things. So living things are constantly battling the loss of energy. They do it through taking in and
organizing other forms of energy. Eating. Breathing.
Drinking. Reading. Well, not only do you eat, but you are
constantly being eaten as well. There are billions of micro-
organisms living in your gastrointestinal system, for instance. You're constantly doing a dance with them. Are
you still with me?"

I dryly told him I thought I could stay conscious until
he finished his train of thought.

"As you know, I've developed techniques and equipment
which lets me identify subtle-energy frequencies. I can do
this to the point where I can very accurately pinpoint many
thousands of different frequency imbalances. I can also remove these imbalances if experience has shown they are not
desirable for the well-being of the person whose subtle-
energy I am examining. This has given me a picture of
what's going on around us that is somewhat unique: I see
the world as an infinite interplay of subtle-energetic forces.
Through careful manipulation of these forces, we can
achieve an edge in the battle of survival. We can experience
enhanced well-being on every level if we remove subtle-
energy blockages which impede our natural ability to keep
ourselves in top condition. This may be experienced physically, mentally, emotionally, spiritually. As we remove
negative frequencies from our energetic field, we become
more and more able to express our lives fully and completely. This means different things to different people, of
course. To one person it may mean a better game of tennis,
another may find they think more clearly or are more able

to achieve a sense of flow when they do their work, yet another may find they their family more fully. It may mean a greater sense of present-ness to what is going on around them. It's a very individual thing."

I had followed along pretty well, but I was still stuck. "How does this relate to disease?"

"I'll cover it again for you," Max said, patiently. "I'm not talking about disease directly, because *I don't claim to detect or correct disease*. The way disease is identified has nothing to do with my work. It is interesting though that many of the people who have been my clients have found that they haven't needed to be treated for disease very often, if at all. It seems that when the body's energetic potential is unleashed through the removal of negative frequencies, subtle-energy frequencies which have been found to be detrimental to our well-being, the body seems stronger and more able to use its own inner wisdom, its own immune capabilities, to fight off disease. And that's where we came in on this digression:

"Remember you were asking me about why I'm out here and what I'm doing? Well, I am convinced that medicine is losing the battle against disease. Maybe this is because the diseases themselves are getting stronger. It's impossible to say. But what I do know is that most people seem to have constant low-level illness."

This seemed true enough. I often felt run-down for weeks at a stretch, until I went to Max and got balanced. Most people I knew had a constant cough or a constant headache or complained that they didn't have any energy. Oddly, if I complained of my own general malaise, many

people would reply somewhat imperiously that they felt
fine; however, on closer questioning they'd reveal that
muscle pain plagued them, or arthritis-like joint pain, or
low-grade fever, or migraines. It had gotten to the point
where everyone was simply living with these symptoms as if
they were an expected part of life, instead of impediments
on the road to true well-being.

"That's exactly what I'm talking about," Max affirmed.
"And the number of people that want energetic balancing
has increased way beyond my ability to provide it. Having
a team of trained testers in Sanctuary is the only way I can
begin to satisfy people's need for this.

"And I don't think it's really a medical issue. It's more
fundamental than that. I think of it as energetic dysfunction, more on a spiritual level than a physical one. But remember, I didn't coin the phrase 'The spirit devours the
flesh.' Routinely, my clients would come in with long lists
of physical, mental and emotional symptoms. When I
tested them, they often would turn out to exhibit a huge
range of frequencies associated with serious illnesses, like
Marburg or HIV or Idiopathic CD-4 or progressive multi-
focal leukoencephalopathy. They'll never get a medical diagnosis of these things and I'm not claiming they have them
medically. But when the frequencies go away, they get a
dramatic improvement in their well-being. Depression, for
instance, is very commonly accompanied by the frequencies
associated with TB. When I rebalance them to remove
those frequencies, the depression goes away."

"A common problem people have in their thinking,"
Max said, "is that they think the world has to be simple and

obvious. It's easy to believe that 'mechanistic determinism' — the Newtonian world view where the universe is a giant clockworks and everything is somehow orderly and predictable — is real. But remember, modern quantum physics has gone so far beyond Newton that for some kinds of thinking he's hardly even relevant anymore. In the quantum universe, energy is all there is. Energy obeys certain laws, most of the time. And that's the key. When we talk about energy, we are talking about something that is not predictable other than by statistical probability. And with probability, any individual event may turn out any which way. Over a large number of events, we can make good guesses as to the distribution of outcomes, but each single event is its own unpredictable phenomenon all to itself. That's why casinos get queasy when somebody hits a winning streak. They believe in the odds in the long run, but they hate when an event follows the line of improbability. And as it happens, since everything is energy (according to physicists and I think they're right) then everything is subject to the laws of quantum physics. That includes both the subatomic and atomic levels as well as larger objects. And the weird things about those laws is that they are themselves not internally consistent."

He paused and I got the feeling this was a crucial point.

"What inconsistencies?" I probed.

"That's a big subject," Max replied, "perhaps best left to another conversation. For now, let's say that..." He hesitated again, as if weighing whether he should tell me this secret.

"What?" I pressed impatiently.

"The inconsistencies seem to indicate that consciousness is the basic building block of matter, that the entire universe is conscious. In fact, I believe that is ultimately why energetic balancing works and why the use of photographs for testing and imprinting works. And that's why I call my testing apparatus a 'Quantum-Consciousness Evaluation Device' and I think of subtle-energy as Quantum Consciousness Units."

"Quantum-Consciousness Evaluation Device?" I pondered.

"QED," Max smiled. "From the Latin *'Quod erat demonstrandum'* — meaning 'that which is to be shown or demonstrated.'"

"Is the name yet another coincidence?" I asked, laughing.

"Not coincidence," Max corrected. "Synchronicity."

"So how would physics explain the relationship between energetic imbalance and disease?" I wondered.

"The first thing you must understand is that one who practices physics is a physicist — not a physician," Max said. The closest we might come in this discussion to comparing subtle-energy frequencies with actual disease is in the comparison between light viewed as a wave and as a particle. The photon, which is thought of as a particle of light, has properties of both a wave and a particle at the same time. The things which they have found out about the behavior of photons shows that when you identify the particle of light, you lose the ability to identify the wave of light. And if you examine the wave, you cannot identify the particle."

I had a hard time grasping this, too, and he reminded me that Niels Bohr, the father of the atom, the man who had postulated and identified what is now commonly accepted as the structure of that building block of matter, said "Those who are not shocked when they first come across quantum theory cannot possibly have understood it."

"It's as if a chemist tried to figure out how a television set works. Of course, there are many chemicals in a television set, and you might actually be able to tune in a TV station by chemically manipulating the television. But basically the television is an energetic device. So it is with the human organism. We are actually highly complex energetic entities. Most of us are fully convinced only of our solid physicality. Many philosophers have endlessly debated the nature of mind and thought and emotion and spirit as well as the nature of the body, but they don't have a deep enough grasp on most of these things.

"Think about electricity. The early experimenters of the 18th and 19th centuries debated what kind of thing it was. They thought it was a fluid or an ether, whatever they meant by those things. They invented strange devices that manifested aspects of electricity and they came up with words to describe those things. But because the common man had no idea what they were doing or dealing with, those words were mysterious and difficult to understand. Today, when the nature of electricity has been more clearly defined and manifestations of electricity can be seen all around us, many people grasp the specialized language that describes electrical activity.

"Electricity is a good case in point for people who are skeptical about the existence of things that can't be seen. Along with x-rays and atomic radiation and radio waves among many other things, it is an example of something that not long ago was little known or unknown, and mostly useless, though subsequent work exploring the use of these things has yielded everything from the atom bomb and nuclear power to the personal stereo and the cellular phone. The work I do is in the same vein: It has to do with energy. That energy is of a type which few people currently are aware of, yet it is the energy that makes up all things."

Max stopped for a second while I reflected, trying to hold the pieces of everything he was saying in some kind of order, like a jigsaw puzzle, so I could see the whole picture. Then he started talking again.

"Einstein and his peers were the ones that made the key scientific breakthroughs that underlie my work. As it happens, the work they did was complementary to other research done by people in many esoteric disciplines, including meditation and spirituality and psychology and other even more obscure fields. Eventually the physicists saw something as transcendental as any moment of enlightenment: Everything is energy. I'll repeat that: *Everything is energy*.

"Yes, but isn't that kind of abstract?" I asked. "What can we actually *do* with that information?"

"Information is energy, too," Max replied, "And for starters, I've been able to use that idea to examine the energetic nature of many things. Building upon the work of those before me, I've managed to develop a lucid system of energetic analysis which detects subtle-energy imbalances. For years, I've been able to observe the changes that happen in people when their energetic imbalances are removed. These changes include huge shifts in their sense of well-being, their ability to enjoy life, to adapt to changes, to think more clearly, to love more deeply, to release unproductive and uncomfortable patterns in their lives. They go from being the unwitting victims of subtle forces to being the self-actuated creative force in their lives."

I realized I was feeling a little off-kilter as we spoke.

"Do you mind checking me?" I asked, sticking out my thumb.

He laughed. "That's the bottom line, isn't it?"

We sat down to the machine, ran through an evaluation. He found frequencies for a type of pollen and some sinus imbalances.

Max laughed again and said, "I'll bet it's in our collective noses."

Then, putting his own photograph in the circuit, he used my thumb to test himself. He had the same frequency imbalance I did. Our pictures went onto an imprinting machine. Less then an hour later, both of us felt fine.

Jane's Second Re-evaluation

IT WAS hard to believe that Jane was the same person Max had tested a month earlier. She was putting on weight, not in the sense of getting fat, but in the sense of filling out the sagging skin which hung from her bones. Her face was fleshing out again and her eyes had a sparkle to them. Even her hair was starting to grow back. She had given up her wig and was letting the crew-cut length hair show.

Max began testing. Menu after menu, all we heard was the high-pitched sound indicating that the frequencies he was testing weren't present. He looked up from the machine.

"I need to know what 'yes' looks like," he said.

He flipped to a screen, selected a frequency and elicited the familiar low-toned positive.

"What's that?" Jane asked. "Is it cancer?"

"I'm not going to bore you again with the fact that I don't identify cancer," Max said.

"Don't play games with me, Max," Jane said. "What did you find?"

"The computer says you're a woman," Max answered. "On the other hand, it says you're not..." He tested a different frequency and we heard the high-pitched tone, "a man."

Jane looked appropriately baffled.

"It's simple," Max said, showing her the screen where it indicated Male/Female. "Everything is yes or no. 'Maybe' is unacceptable. Now watch."

He tested 'Female' sex again and got a low-pitched response. And, of course, the high-pitched negative response on 'Male' sex.

He paged to the malignancy-frequency trays. Page after page yielded consistent results: High-pitched negatives. He then went individually to each of the frequencies that had been positive. Again, negative.

"Now let's look at the hereditary frequencies," he said.

Paging through the malignancy screens, he still could find no hits.

Max turned to Jane. "The frequency of malignancy in you is gone, both actively and hereditarily."

Jane struggled to keep her composure, failed, made a small choking sound, then broke out in tears. Max squeezed her hand as she sobbed. Terry threw her arms around me and buried her face in my neck. I could feel the tears running down her cheek as I held her in return.

"I knew it," Jane sobbed. "I could feel it leave." She turned to Max. "It was like I knew I had cancer before my doctor ever told me. Somehow. And in that same way, I knew it was gone before I came in here today."

"Of course you did," Max replied solemnly. "You know everything about yourself."

He waited patiently for Jane's weeping to subside.

"I don't want to interrupt our celebration," Max said. "But there's always more."

A worried frown creased Jane's brow.

Max put up a hand to calm her. "I don't make the rules," he said. "I just know them. And since there's always more, there is more beyond your cancer frequencies."

She nodded.

"Would you like to see what else is wrong with you?" he asked.

"Yes." Jane's voice cracked.

"To begin with, let's see what frequencies you've inherited besides cancer," Max said.

He set the machine to the right pages and began testing. Quickly we heard the familiar low-toned whine.

"You have the frequency of a party animal in your family tree," Max said. "Syphilis."

Jane was aghast. "I've never had syphilis."

"You never *didn't* have it," Max responded. "The problem is, you didn't even enjoy getting it. Show me your teeth."

With a little more coaxing from Max, Jane said, "I feel like a horse," and sort of smiled.

"That frequency usually causes crooked or gapped teeth," Max told her. "But yours look pretty good."

"I wore braces for years," Jane muttered, a little embarrassed.

"I find this frequency in almost everyone," he said.

"Do you know who gave it to me?" Jane wondered.

Max tested. "Your father."

"But my father was..."

Max interrupted her. "Just wait a minute. He inherited it from..." More testing. "His mother."

"My grandmother!" Jane exclaimed. "I don't —"

"Who also inherited it from... her mother... who got it actively from... a man, who got it actively from... a woman." Max stopped. "So now we see where it began."

"Where did the woman get it?" Terry piped in, stepping right into Max's trap.

"I don't think that's relevant," said Max. "It always starts with a woman. You can read about it in Genesis."

The room was a predictable mixture of laughter and indignation, divided perfectly on the gender line.

"Let's finish testing Jane," Max said innocently, turning his attention back to the computer.

Max applied the probe, which elicited a low-toned sound. He said to Jane, "You have the frequency of a type of hereditary tuberculosis in the pancreas. You're probably a sugar addict."

Jane nodded.

"If this frequency persists, it won't be long before you'll show the frequency of diabetes."

"My mother was diabetic," she said.

Max replied with the familiar, "It'll be gone in a month," and added, "And I'd expect your sugar craving will go along with it."

He continued through the rest of the balancing regimen, coming up with several additional, though less severe, imbalances. Jane readily acknowledged each one as Max described the associated consequences:

"Your nose is always stuffed up... You have a chronic itch... in the groin... Your eyes are very sensitive to light... You've got a short fuse, quick to anger... Here's one you might not know about, unless you're told by either someone you sleep with or your dentist — or of course if you sleep with your dentist..."

"I don't sleep with my dentist." Jane snapped. "What are you getting at?"

"You grind your teeth at night," he told her.

Finally there were no more low-tones. Jane had revealed everything she could about herself at the moment.

Jane looked at Max. "How can you know so much about me?"

"I don't know anything other than what you've told me," Max said. "You, on the other hand, know *everything* about you. The object of all of this is to make your knowledge conscious. But, then, that's the object of life, isn't it?"

The Thumb Chronicles
Part II

"IT'S ALWAYS ABOUT CONSCIOUS-NESS," Max reminded me as we sat down to another session of Tester and Thumb. "It's about being able to place your awareness in the right place at the right time. In the case of energetic balancing, once the disturbance is identified, once it comes to consciousness, to conscious awareness, then the self, the higher self, the organizing principle in you knows what to do to make it right. What often happens to people is they get stuck on symptoms and try to fix those. But the real action is somewhere else."

"Like a magician redirecting the attention of his audience so they won't see him palm the card?" I asked.

"Let's say it's like trying to re-align a crooked door, when the problem is that the foundation has settled," he suggested.

*   *   *

We talked about times when the moment a frequency imbalance was identified, it disappeared. I remembered a number of times when a headache had vanished the moment Max gave it a name.

Recently, he'd done work on my emotional balance and those frequencies behaved similarly. Sometimes I'd wait a day or two for results, other times I'd find that a negative emotion would be gone as soon as its vibrational name was spoken. At first I was afraid to mention it, thinking it was too weird. But everyone at Sanctuary was having experiences like that. Working through physical, emotional and spiritual imbalances in this way had an effect that seemed like lifetimes of evolution could be traversed in a week.

His explanation was, as usual, mind-boggling:

"Often, once a frequency is 'found-out,'" Max offered, "it seems to lose its secure domain and just leaves."

"Leaves?" I wasn't sure what he was saying.

Max looked me square in the eye. "It voluntarily and volitionally departs when it knows it has been discovered."

"It *knows?*" I asked, incredulous.

"*It knows,*" Max confirmed. "Remember: *everything is alive*. Everything is conscious. $E=mc^2$. Everything is energy. *You* are energy. Thus you are a part of everything — an inseparable part. You have consciousness. So, what makes you think that other parts of the 'everything' aren't as conscious as you?"

"*More* conscious, I would hope," I joked.

Max didn't laugh. "Interesting you should say that," he noted, "because I believe that these frequencies identify entities which are totally conscious — far more than us, I think, because they are aware of our thoughts, but the converse is not true... at least until we find the suckers."

✳   ✳   ✳

Max pointed out that not everything went away instantaneously. This was brought home by occasional bouts of imbalance which persisted for several days. The usual pattern was that specific discomforts seemed to remain, with only minor shifts, though repeated checking showed different frequency imbalances as the cause. Usually in these circumstances, there were slight breaks in the discomfort as a given frequency disappeared, a new frequency would set in and the discomfort would return.

Most of the time, energetic imbalances were gone very quickly, but sometimes an attack like that would last for several days, though I had only had this happen three or four times in the years I had been through energetic balancing.

"These situations happen when a person has an energetic weakness which makes them vulnerable to attack in a certain area," Max explained. "The problem is caused by the continued presence of a fundamental underlying imbalance, which is hereditary and which is one's *vulnerability* with a capital V. Imbalances seek that vulnerability and will find it. It is in accordance with the most basic law of the universe: Survival. It would be idiotic to attack your strength.

You would overcome the attack and in the process become stronger. As long as your weakness remains, that will be the point of entry for any imbalance. Furthermore, even though each imbalance is totally different, subjectively you'll perceive them as being the same. That's because what you're really perceiving is your fundamental weakness. And that is why energetic work is pointless without addressing the deepest hereditary, ancestral imbalances."

"I've been checked many times for hereditary imbalances," I pointed out.

"And sometimes we come across one that wasn't detectable before," Max said. "Either because I've developed a new way of looking for it, or because *you* changed in a way that made the imbalance detectable and correctable. Remember Terry Fisher Virus number one? I was not capable of finding that frequency in the past, because I was only capable of checking against known frequencies. Now I can find previously unknown frequencies. Of course, TFV1 is now a known frequency and I'll find it easily if it appears in others. In fact, I've already found it several times."

"Is being unknown the only factor that makes something undetectable?" I asked.

"I just told you that these imbalances are often conscious energetic entities."

I nodded.

"These entities have the ability and the motivation to *hide*," he said.

I remembered him talking to Jane about her cancer hiding. "But you found it," I said.

"*That* time. I have missed things in the past and some-times still miss them when they hide successfully. But I never give up. And once I find them, I also expose their method and manner of hiding. This means they will never be able to successfully use that method again. Just as TFV1 is in the permanent database, so is every method these fre-quencies use to avoid being detected. If you beat a com-puter at chess, you will never beat it the same way again if the program remembers the game. My computer remem-bers every game.

"I had a very difficult time finding the frequency of can-cer in a client of mine. I spent hours looking. But once I found it, I immediately tested his identical twin brother. It took me thirty seconds to find it in him."

*   *   *

As we started testing again, Max showed me some new applications for energetic balancing. Instead of checking for imbalances and removing them, Max was checking people who were currently not experiencing imbalances, looking for ways to further enhance well-being.

Max had five pictures to check.

"What are we looking for?" I asked.

"What's *right*," said Max.

"Well, if it ain't broke..." I began.

"These five people have the highest life force of any I've ever checked," Max told me. "Higher than yours or mine. Is that acceptable to you?"

"It's intolerable," I answered.

"Then let's find the difference between them and the rest of us," he said.

Over the course of the next few hours, we switched pictures, switched trays, compared and contrasted.

Finally, Max said, "They all have one thing in common that none of us have."

He ran through the trays, and selected a new frequency he had isolated. He got a hit. He checked its energetic potency.

"They have this frequency at an extremely high level," he said.

"Can't we just provide that frequency to the rest of us?" I asked.

"There are still more 'whys' to ask," he replied. "What makes them maintain that level? How can we initiate that change in others?"

By the end of the day, he had figured it out.

"Let's find out what this frequency will do for *you*, for example."

He tested and after a while printed out the effects of his new frequency on me. They were: accelerate cell repair and regeneration; increase mental vitality; increase physical vitality; relieve nervous tension; increase white light; increase systemic immunity.

"Do you want some?" he asked.

I grabbed my picture, put it on an imprinter and dialed in the frequency.

"This is now *my* computer," I said. "I want my picture there permanently."

Max did some more checking and said, "Not necessary. You can take drops three times a day and get the same effect."

"Either way," I replied, "I'm kind of in a rush. While we sit here talking, I'm aging and you're callously indifferent to my plight."

"We can start immediately, if you insist," Max told me.

"I insist."

"But before we begin imprinting, you may want to add a few other frequencies."

"Such as?"

"One to retard the aging process. Another to actually lower your biological age."

"Perfect," I answered. "Put 'em all in."

As I watched him add the frequencies to the imprint tray, I wondered, "Do these frequencies work the same for everybody?"

"Good question," he said, picking up the probe.

We checked the frequency on some other people. For some frequencies, the results were the consistent for each person, but other frequencies turned out to be useful for one person and not useful for another. For each person who wouldn't respond to a given frequency, Max worked out another frequency that would produce the desired result.

"That's why people should be rechecked periodically," Max said. "The database is constantly changing. What we just learned is now in the permanent database, including not just the specific frequencies that work for everybody, but the unique personal frequencies as well."

"Could this be the legendary fountain of youth?" I asked.

"Not by itself," Max said. "But used in addition to other energetic means, like eliminating hereditary imbalances which activate as the body gets older, the body becomes better able to regenerate itself on the cellular level. It maintains, rather than disintegrates, itself. Looking at the process microbiologically, we can remove the frequencies of negative telomerase, for example those specific to the frequency of malignancy."

"I read about telomerase and telomeres," I said. "Telomeres are generated when DNA splits during cell reproduction. They protect the DNA from getting damaged. And telomerase causes the telomeres to be regenerated so the cell can safely split again. As I understand it, that's what makes cancer cells keep reproducing."

"That's what I meant by negative telomerase," Max nodded. "But it doesn't address aging unless you see death as an acceptable means of halting the aging process. The second task is to find a frequency which can help the body generate telomerase for *healthy* cells. That's the fountain of youth."

"Is this a new idea?" I asked.

"No," he said. "It's just a restatement for those who are uncomfortable talking about energy."

*   *   *

Another unusual testing situation I witnessed was of a couple who on the surface seemed to be absolutely compatible, physically, emotionally and intellectually. They found themselves powerless against a growing hostility directed at one another.

On the tray for compatibility, Max found they indeed had incompatibilities. But the cause was not emotional. It turned out they each had a polarity frequency which was negative and incompatible with the other. Max tested for a remedy that would alter that polarity and bring the couple back into balance with one another. It turned out to be a gem elixir, in this case onyx.

"Could this have been resolved through therapy?" I wondered.

"I didn't check that," Max said. "But in this case, onyx elixir was indicated as the most effective remedy. But that's only in their case. I wouldn't suggest you give onyx to an attractive woman you meet at a party. It might make her hate you. Remember that for many imbalances, energetic analysis often reveals that each person requires a completely different balancing frequency from every other person with that imbalance. Every person is unique, with his or her own innate energetic frequencies, imbalances and requirements."

In subsequent compatibility testing, the effective frequency was that of a color. Other times, it was a unique frequency without an existing name, i.e. one not associated with any known substance or thing. Sometimes it was a frequency Max had previously identified as "Effective frequency for promoting compatibility."

*   *   *

On one occasion, a member of the Choir, using my thumb, stopped after about a minute. He turned to Max and said, "He doesn't pass the Eligibility Evaluation."

He was testing the picture of a key employee, sent in by Kurt, a Sanctuary member who was the head of a large corporation. The first thing that came up positive was "Subject Unaware of Energetic Evaluation."

Max immediately had Jennifer call Kurt to find out why they were testing someone who hadn't asked for it.

"This guy has done such a great job," he told her. "Now he just can't get anything done. Something's got to be wrong with him and I want to help him."

"But does he want to be helped?" Jennifer asked.

"Well," Kurt replied, "I've offered it to him several times and he keeps saying he'll think about it. But meanwhile he's going downhill. It was a decision I felt I had to make."

"It was a decision you *couldn't* make," Jennifer told him. "You could only offer. It's up to him to accept or reject that offer."

As it turned out, Kurt paid for regular energetic balancing for several of his key employees and paid for testing on an as-needed basis for many others. He felt that the cost was a small investment to ensure that his employees would have less down time and would function at peak levels. His employees also considered it an extraordinary benefit. But until now, they had all specifically agreed to be tested.

"You don't have to tell me what you found," Kurt said.

"We don't tell you that anyway," Jennifer told him. "You know that. But testing and re-balancing a person without their consent is out of the question. In fact, we consider it to be an intrusion and highly unethical."

"I thought I was giving him a gift," Kurt lamented.

"Max isn't questioning your motive," Jennifer said. "Nevertheless, it's an invasion of his privacy. Please don't let it happen again."

She packed up the picture and mailed it back to Kurt.

"Actually," Jennifer said, "this is an ongoing problem. Especially with couples who want to have a child. If one person has gotten rid of all his energetic imbalances, but the other hasn't, the 'clean' one will often ask us to take care of the other partner, without his or her knowledge, so that their baby won't have the hereditary weaknesses that have run in either family."

"Would you ever do that?" I asked.

"Only if the untested person was Jennifer," Max joked. "We make a point of intruding on each other. Otherwise, as usual, we need the explicit permission of the person being evaluated."

"What about the child?" I pressed.

"Once they have the baby," Max said, "it only takes one parent to send me the picture and request energetic balancing."

Kurt's company was only one example of many Sanctuary members who used energetic balancing via standing orders to be checked weekly and in some cases, even daily. In the case of one woman who had a standing order for daily balancing, I heard Max ask if she felt she needed to be checked.

Her answer was, "I feel fine, but I want the security of knowing that whatever imbalances I might get are taken care of as soon as possible. I don't care about the cost. As far as I am concerned, the main benefit to having money is to be able to ensure my well-being. This is the most effective way I've ever seen to do that."

Max felt that it wasn't necessary to be evaluated on a daily basis, though most of us at Sanctuary were. We felt it was a perk, and helped us avoid discomfort. Max pointed out that *the most important function of energetic balancing was to eliminate the imbalances which would persist without energetic intervention,* not to help us overcome the things we would easily overcome on our own.

Of course, we had a stock answer: "We won't know which ones we have without testing, will we?"

It was one of the few times I'd seen Max give up trying to convince us of his point of view. He knew when he was beaten.

"How often would you recommend energetic balancing?" I asked, trying to ascertain a more practical timeline.

"It depends on the individual," he replied. "If you feel fine, I'd recommend being tested every few months to take advantage of changes in the technology and new energetic information, such as newly-found frequencies that may inhibit aging. Otherwise, the normal routine is that a person follows our Initial Energetic Protocol, which includes the Initial Comprehensive Evaluation, two follow-up evaluations, then the Specific Comprehensive Evaluation — which is structured entirely with respect to the weaknesses, imbalances and complaints that the member feels are still remaining — and its mandatory follow-up. These, along with two optional follow-ups included as part of the Initial Energetic Protocol, will uncover and eliminate most energetic imbalances. Once this regimen has been concluded, an as-needed basis is fine unless you're interested in doing more-subtle work, which *I* think is a great idea, but not everybody does. Some people are happy achieving a state of relative comfort, others are compelled to achieve their full potential, their maximum state of consciousness."

"More-subtle work?" My curiousity was aroused. "Like what?"

"Cleansing of the subtle bodies, for instance," Max replied.

"What good does it do?" I wondered.

"Freedom," he said.

"From what?"

"True freedom isn't *from*," he said. "It's *to*. As in 'the freedom to...' where you fill in the blanks yourself, instead of having them filled in for you by the history of your own limitations."

*   *   *

Another rejection occurred for a completely different reason. Max was re-checking a Sanctuary member who had called in to complain that energetic rebalancing wasn't helping her. Looking through the woman's record, Max noted the frequencies found when she received an evaluation three weeks earlier. He flipped her photograph on the tray and steadily checked each frequency again.

"Watch this," he indicated the screen. "Notice that some of these frequencies — like this one — are gone. Others..." He flipped to another screen, pressed the probe to my thumb again. "Are still around."

I didn't know what he was getting at. "So it's taking longer to remove those frequencies?" I asked.

He shook his head. "Some things *do* take longer to release than others."

"Hereditary imbalances, for example?"

"For example," he agreed. "Though there are some frequencies that are not hereditary that can take a long time to remove. But that's not what's happening here."

He called up the list of frequencies which he found were still present, then referred to the record.

"Notice that some frequencies were rebalanced photographically and we sent her energetic solutions to deal with the others." He indicated the record. "All the photographically-balanced frequencies are gone. But none of the solution-balanced frequencies are gone."

"So the solutions didn't work?" I concluded.

"That's hard to believe," he replied. "But then again, we don't have to believe. We can check."

He abused my thumb some more, measuring the energetic level of each of the remaining frequencies.

"There," he indicated. "A frequency does not exist at that level in nature. It indicates that the energetic solutions — *were* working."

"Well, what happened?" I asked.

"This," he said.

He flipped to a screen I hadn't seen before and focused the selection on a particular frequency. He pressed the probe to my thumb. It came up positive.

I looked at the selection. It was the frequency for "not taking energetic solution."

Max had a look on his face I rarely, if ever, saw: a combination of hurt, anger and frustration.

"So they didn't take their drops," I said. "So what? It's their life, their karma."

"Ultimately you're right, of course," Max said. "And as the German philosopher, Schiller, said, 'Against stupidity, the gods themselves labor in vain.' But the problem is that *I'm* blamed and my work is denigrated for her failure to follow directions."

"Non-compliance," I said, using the buzzword that physicians used to refer to patients who didn't take their prescribed medications.

"There are a lot of differences between what I do and what doctors do," Max grimaced. "First of all, as you know, energetic balancing is neither a treatment nor a cure for disease. But, on one hand, doctors are routinely forgiven for their failures. People will return to their physician again and again, even if their conditions don't respond to the prescribed treatments, even if they are made worse by those treatments. And they don't think their doctors have failed — they just let them keep on trying. Yet, on the other hand, these same people will claim energetic balancing failed if they don't have immediate results from rebalancing. They don't expect their doctor to perform miracles, but they expect me to perform them. And they expect to be cured of their diseases, even though they've been told over and over and have signed agreements stating that energetic balancing is not a cure for disease. And then they demand energetic balancing be effective whether they take their drops or not. These same people wouldn't dream of telling their physician

'I didn't take the antibiotic, how come I still have the infection.'"

"They want a *Deus ex machina* ending," I suggested, quoting a Latin term meaning "God comes out of the machine," used in storytelling to describe a certain kind of bad resolution to a drama, first popularized by the ancient Greek playwrights, in which the conflicts in the play would be resolved by the gods showing up and smiting the bad guys.

Max smiled. "I guess I'll have to play God."

Then he picked up the phone and dialed the woman we had just checked. He told her what we found. She acknowledged that she had taken the drops for "perhaps a day" but had discontinued because of her "busy schedule."

"Besides," she added, "I didn't think they were working."

Max was quiet for a moment. Then: "Based on what you're telling me," he said into the phone again, "I have to agree with your conclusion: What we do *doesn't* work for you. Therefore Sanctuary will not do energetic balancing for you, now or in the future."

I heard a sharp protest from the tinny handset speaker.

"Please understand," Max told her, "I can accept failing in what I do. It only makes me try harder. But I will not fail because you decided you know best about energetic balancing. I think you've sent us a clear message that this work isn't for you."

He hung up the phone.

"Isn't that a little strong?" I asked.

"What's the point in continuing with her if she's not going to cooperate?" he asked. It's her choice and I respect her right to make it. And there are many like her: people who don't take their drops, who don't do follow-up evaluations when they are required by their specific imbalance. But I am not willing to waste our energy, our time and our resources on those people, when there are so many others pleading for time with our testers."

Max handed the woman's paperwork to Jennifer. "Please send her our form letter about energetic balancing not being appropriate for her lifestyle."

*   *   *

One day, I was a whale. It turned out one of Max's friends who belonged to Sanctuary was the head of a committee to save an ailing whale. It was suffering from a severe skin problem, losing weight rapidly and, according to the veterinarians in attendance, was approaching critical condition.

Max said to me, "Let me have your flipper."

I tried to fight the irresistible impulse to flip him off, but lost.

"Wrong one," he said without blinking and took my thumb.

We did a thorough evaluation and promptly put the whale's picture on the imprint tray. It took about a week before Max's friend called up, deliriously happy, to report that the skin problem was almost completely gone and he was eating... like a whale. As it turned out, in less than a year he gained twenty-five hundred pounds, back to his normal weight.

My thumb had also been cats, dogs and horses. The frequencies found in these animals were for the most part the same as those found in humans. Most important, animals were able to benefit from balancing energies to achieve greater well-being as reported by their owners.

In one horse, we found the frequency of diabetes. Once it was corrected, she stopped trying to throw her rider. A dog stopped biting people when the frequency of his encephalitis was removed. Another dog lacked sufficient life-force to be treated and, sadly enough, died from cancer a few days later. Interestingly enough, there seemed to be no difference in the range of energetic imbalances which affected humans and animals. But, not surprisingly, pet owners had far more frequencies of "animal diseases" than people who didn't have much contact with animals.

Max responded to this observation by saying that in the past it was common and prevalent to not allow pets in the house, but now we're enlightened, so we don't know any better.

Jennifer bristled and pointed out that their cat slept in bed with her and Max... Under the covers. And it was going to continue to do so.

Once again, Max knew when he was beaten.

*   *   *

I was called in as an "emergency thumb." A member's baby was in the hospital with a serious lung problem which the doctors could not identify. They had warned the father that there was a good chance they would lose the baby. Antibiotics had failed. Nothing else they tried was effective and, though the mother was always vehemently against energetic analysis for herself and her children, the father, who happily and regularly used energetic balancing services himself, was frantic. He faxed us a picture of the baby.

Max and I quickly went to work. Rather, Max and my thumb quickly went to work. He measured the baby's life force, which was low, and then found the frequency for the baby's potential early demise. Within five minutes, Max identified a serious frequency imbalance and noted its high potential for fatality. The baby's faxed photo was placed on the tray, while we monitored a photocopy of the fax.

It took about fifteen minutes for the baby's life force to go above the critical range, and about an hour for her life force to be normal.

Shortly thereafter, the father called again and told Max, "Forget about checking the baby, she's doing fine. The doctors are congratulating themselves. They say they've beaten it. And, as you know, my wife would rather not have energetic frequencies used on our baby."

"Too late," Max told him, and explained what had transpired. "But the baby is fine and that's all that really matters," he finished.

The father was quiet for a moment before disagreeing with Max. "No, that's not all that matters," he said. "The fact is, she's *my* child, too, and I have the right to request your help. My wife has the right to know, of course — and it's time she acknowledged how much you've done for us, now and in the past."

But she did not acknowledge what Max had done until much later, when she finally called for herself.

"I've been diagnosed with cancer," she told him. "I want you to check me."

Max pointed out that she had always had total confidence in her physicians. "I'm neither willing nor able to advise you to abandon their ship," he said.

She persisted, though, and Max capitulated. He found that, apart from her medical diagnosis, she indeed had the *frequency* of cancer as well. He dealt with the imbalance and it was gone in a month.

As her energetic-balancing regimen took her past the cancer frequencies and she shed her other subtle-energy imbalances, she began to radiate her new-found well-being.

Her oncologist, Dr. Walker, watched her change and questioned her at length when she told him she didn't need him anymore.

"What do you mean your cancer is gone?" he asked, disdainfully. "Where did it go?"

"I must have left it in a restaurant," she said cheerfully. "I'm so scatter-brained."

He angrily washed his hands of her.

Subsequently, she spoke to Max, expressing her gratitude and also her embarrassment.

"What can I do to make up for the way I've treated you and spoken of you?" she asked.

"It's simple," Max said. "Just know the truth and tell it. Just make sure it's *your* truth and not one you've been given through dogma, common knowledge or popular opinion. That's all I ask. That's all I can ever ask of anyone."

Her referrals started pouring in to Sanctuary, all of them talking about the remarkable changes they had seen in her.

Max Speaks

ALL OF US were constantly asking Max's opinion. Sometimes he hosted gatherings where he would address some of the more common questions.

Max enjoyed saying "Now that Sanctuary is a church, you feel I'm obligated to pontificate."

He was right.

Exercise, nutrition and common sense

Outside of energetic balance issues, his views generally came down to two things: common sense and responsibility. For example, when asked whether energetic balancing replaced the need for exercise or good nutrition, he began an indignant diatribe:

"You have a cardiovascular system, thus it has to be maintained," he said. "It requires use. Any system in your body that is not used will atrophy, and eventually will no longer function. It's absurd to question whether exercise or intelligent nutrition is desirable: Anyone who wishes to self-destruct will succeed, with or without energetic balancing. Nothing I or anyone else can do will divest you of responsibility for your own life. If you don't want it, don't live it. And don't waste my time.

"There may be underlying energetic causes for destructive lifestyles, such as the frequencies of depression, diabetes, hereditary imbalances, etc. If those frequencies are found, we can remove them, but you will still have to take responsibility for yourself. It is not our aim to enable you to live a long and healthy life lying on a couch eating ice cream and Twinkies. In fact, if you have that need, you are already spiritually bereft. And once again the spirit will devour the flesh.

"It is not the bailiwick of an MD or any other professional to be able to say you must have common sense in your life. I have no doubt someone will ask me if I think that energetically-speaking it's a good idea to vacation in Chernobyl. The question boggles my mind now and will do so then. At some point, when you speak of levels of consciousness, you can also speak of levels of insanity. Unfortunately, they are often synonymous.

"What responsibility means is being your own guru. We can only help you find the way. Any healing, any progress, any hope, any despair is going to come from you. It is *your* energy that matters. I can't give you *my* energy and I wouldn't dream of it. I need it for me. But I can help you find your energy. I'm obligated to help you find it, in any way I can.

*   *   *

Another common set of questions involved environmental toxins.

He considered himself a fundamentalist: "Obviously, prolonged or voluminous exposure to any product that is alien to your body inevitably will result in a toxic state. Because the body rejects that which is not natural to it. How does it reject it? It sees an invading toxin, something that's now resident in your body and makes allergies in response to it, to discourage you from further contact with that thing. Or it makes antibodies against it."

"When you're allergic to something in your own body, isn't that an autoimmune problem?" someone asked him.

"Of course," Max answered. "And, energetically speaking, we find and remove the frequencies of autoimmune problems quite often. But nobody thinks about what they have done to cause these frequencies."

Max continued, "There are other reactions to toxins. Sometimes the body walls them off and encysts them to protect you. It's a valid defense. But sometimes the cyst itself creates an energetic blockage, or perhaps physical. If the cyst results in a little fatty tumor in the arm, that's nothing to consider. If the cyst blocks the sinus and obstructs breathing, the protection your body is giving you can't be viewed positively. But ultimately the culprit isn't the cyst, it's a toxin your body is protecting you against."

"If we're energetically balanced enough, will we transcend these toxins?" was another question from his audience.

"It's not realistic to assume you'll reach a state of harmony where you can ingest and be exposed to poisons and never suffer any ill effects," he replied. "Perhaps that is true at some point in the evolutionary scale — the scale perhaps of the yogis, the Buddha. Perhaps not. I don't know. I know for me, and probably for you, exposure to poison results in toxicity. And it seems to be just ecologically sound to avoid exposure to poisons. And at any level it makes sense to me. For instance, if I need a filling for a tooth, I prefer to have gold used because gold is a trace element in the body, whereas the mercury used in amalgam fillings is not. That's just common sense. It makes sense to cook in iron because iron is a part of the blood, whereas aluminum is not a naturally-ocurring trace element in the body. I don't see any way for the body not to respond to a foreign substance as if it's an invader or an enemy. I don't think this is a matter of medical dispute. It's just good common sense.

"A lot of you probably know that the incidence of Alzheimer's is at an all-time high. Aluminum didn't really exist until around 1940 and Alzheimer's has long been associated with aluminum. Notably, the incidence of Alzheimer's is far greater in advanced countries than in primitive countries, where they still cook primarily with iron. I understand aluminum is lighter, but technology can't replace intelligence. Your life is *your* responsibility."

*   *   *

Probably the single most common question tossed at Max had to do with whether or not someone should go to an MD for a given condition.

Max had a consistent response. "I would never tell you not to go to a doctor, if you feel you need to go. If you feel you have a disease, it's appropriate to go to a medical doctor. But if a doctor can't identify or solve your problem, it's prudent to believe there may be another solution. And that solution may be energetic."

"Would you see a medical doctor?" he was asked.

"Of course," Max answered. "If the circumstances warrant it. If I'm choking on a chicken bone, I'm not going to look for the frequency of 'anti-chicken bone.' I'll want the chicken bone removed immediately. Surgically, if necessary. If I have a disease that will benefit from medical treatment, I'm certainly going to avail myself of that treatment."

In response to a question about whether energetic balancing should be used along with or in addition to medical treatment, Max replied, "I've told you that disease frequencies move into an energetic vacuum. That may also be true of actual diseases. So even if a disease is treated by an MD, it may be in your best interests to identify that vacuum, that is, to identify your vulnerability. Of course, the responsibility for that decision is yours to make."

Someone once told Max that his doctor had told him not to use energetic evaluations because it didn't address his disease.

"Try to imagine the proportion of the world's problems that have come from misquotation and a lack of understanding," Max said. "Most of the conflicts I've had with the medical community came from clients telling doctors I'm treating their diseases and it doesn't seem to matter how many times I correct them. They hear what they want, say what they want and put quotes around it, which don't belong there because they're not my words. I'm willing to take responsibility for my claims, but not the claims of others."

＊　　＊　　＊

Over the course of testing, frequencies of "dread diseases" often came up. Inevitably someone would wring their hands and ask if Max could deal with them. Max was always patient. He methodically checked to see if the frequency was resolvable; inevitably the answer was yes. The only exceptions he seemed to encounter were the frequencies of heavy metal toxicity and systemic parasites.

"Other than those," he explained, "they're all just 'alphabet soup.' Forget about the name. If it's a frequency, and it can be reversed, it'll be gone. It doesn't matter whether it's the frequency of measles, malignancy or HIV. The question is not the *name* of the frequency, but whether it can be reversed. In most cases, the answer is yes... if *you* can do it, if your strength, your life force is adequate."

＊　　＊　　＊

One evening, Doug asked Max about one of the subjects that he had evaluated earlier, a pregnant woman who had asked for an initial evaluation to determine if there were any energetic imbalances in her fetus.

"I was amazed," Doug reported. "We found all sorts of imbalances in the fetus. And not just hereditary ones. How do you reconcile these disease frequencies with the concept of the placental barrier?"

"The answer is provided in your question," Max replied. "These are *frequencies*, and there are no barriers to energy." He smiled: "But, Doug, if my memory serves me correctly, the placental barrier appears to be permeable to anything smaller than a medium-sized rodent. How do you account for the fact that a relatively benign virus like German measles routinely causes birth defects in the fetus? What happened to the placental barrier for Thalidomide babies? Where is the placental barrier for the unborn children of cigarette smokers and people who drink alcohol or take cocaine or crack during their pregnancy? Apparently the placental barrier is highly effective against anything that has no effect on a fetus. But if it *has* an effect, the placental barrier just lays down on the job."

"Uh," Doug muttered, "point taken."

"And how about the blood/brain barrier?" Max continued his roll. "Why is it that a mosquito can bite you on the foot and you can get encephalitis in the brain? How does it get to the brain? And how about syphilis? After it leaves the bloodstream, it enters the spinal cord and brain. Another hypothetical barrier not functioning.

"There's only one barrier I've ever seen that's infallible," he finished. "And that is the barrier of perception."

*   *   *

Pamela asked Max about possible energetic dangers from getting cosmetic surgery.

"There is a protective aura around each of us," Max explained. "It is part of our resistance to pathological frequencies. Surgery — any surgery — causes a breach in that aura, a hole in the protective envelope. Since nature abhors a vacuum, any negative frequency that *can* get in, will. Everyone I've ever tested after surgery has manifested negative frequencies that are normally not found. This is not an argument against surgery. If you need it, or you want it, you should have it. But I believe there's clearly a need for energetic balancing until you have healed, both physically and etherically."

"Would *you* have cosmetic surgery?" she asked.

"I have," he said. "I didn't like wearing glasses so I had my eyes surgically corrected."

"Were there any problems?"

"It was an amazing experience," he continued. "When something enters your nose, you may sneeze and not think much about it, but any negative frequency entering your eye feels like a hot needle. You don't need to wonder if something's wrong. You *know*, instantly. The first day or two after surgery I had to remove negative frequencies from my cornea a dozen times. After that they were more superficial, in the lens, and they were less frequent. Within a week, my protection was back and I was able to stop checking. Then I had to go through the same thing with the other eye. When I went back to the surgeon for follow-up visits, both times, he was absolutely astounded. Everyone else who had the same surgery the same day was sitting around his waiting room with swollen faces and pus dripping from their eyes. I was fine. He told me I must be bionic. I didn't bother to let him know how many times I had to work on myself, how many hot needles I felt. Of course, in my case, none of the imbalances lasted more than fifteen minutes." He smiled. "It's one of the perks of doing what I do."

"How about emotional trauma?" Pamela asked.

"There's no difference," he replied. "Your body can make your mind sick or vice-versa. A negative emotional state creates vulnerability. People who read auras see the change, the weakness, caused by emotional imbalance. Energetically, we can correct the imbalance. When the imbalance is removed, the aura gets stronger. It, like your body, has its own wisdom, its own ability to heal."

*   *   *

"Are all frequency imbalances conscious?" I asked him, thinking about what he had told me about frequencies being conscious entities.

"*Everything* is conscious," he said. "The question you're really asking is whether something is consciously affecting you to your detriment. If so, you can construe that as an attack and defend yourself in any way you can. There are two things to consider: First of all, what is it about *you* that has invited a negative influence you are unable to overcome? Only consciousness, true consciousness, will tell you that. Energetic testing is our church's form of confession. *You* have all the answers. We work together to raise them to a conscious level. And when we say you invited the negative influence, I'm not necessarily talking about 'sin' or 'transgression' or even 'lifestyle.' The invitation may be a hereditary imbalance. Another word for it might be 'karma.' Whatever you want to call it, we find and remove negative frequencies which hinder your defense and your growth."

"If energetic testing is our form of confession," I asked, "then is energetic imprinting our form of prayer?"

"Let's just say it's our mantra," Max answered. "Okay," he continued, "our first factor is *you*. The second factor is *it*. If a frequency is secure in you, if it wants to stay in you, even if it will ultimately kill you, its innate intelligence will make it hide to avoid detection until it's strong enough that it feels you are unable to remove it. It *has* to hide if it wants to survive within you. And *everything* wants to survive. Once it has gathered enough strength, at your expense, it no longer has to hide. And it will always make itself obvious, one way or another, if it feels that it is invulnerable to you, beyond your ability to control it. The frequency now views *you* as a manifestation of *it*.

"I view that behavior as conscious, devious and malevolent. Often, *it* will win and you will lose — unless you are able to focus *all* your energy to overcome it. That is precisely what our work enables you to do."

The End of the
Thumb Chronicles

A CLIENT CALLED with agonizing back pain which could only be treated surgically. But he was calling on a satellite phone from a film shoot on location in Africa and the pain medication he was taking prevented him from working. Obviously, there was no way Max could energetically correct the imbalance of a herniated disc, but we looked for the frequency of his pain, figured out a balancing energy that would stop it and put him on a tray. He called back the next day, ecstatic. He had stopped taking the pain killers and, for the first time in weeks, he had been able to both work and rest.

"I told my surgeon," he said, "and he wanted to know if he could get some of that energetic frequency for his other patients."

Max told him there was no point. The frequency was targeted to eliminate the specific frequency of *his* specific pain.

"Is there a general frequency for menstrual cramps?" Terry asked.

"I have some right here in my purse," Jennifer spoke up.

"I know just how you feel," Max said.

The women looked at him, humorlessly.

*   *   *

We were testing and my thumb wasn't cooperating. The entire morning, Suzanne, my *tester du jour*, had been pulling at it, trying to get it to behave. She pulled it, it hurt, I pulled back. We were both irritated.

After lunch, I had a new tester, Doug, which was just fine with me. The problem persisted. My thumb was stiff.

Doug began to grumble and actually said to me, "Relax."

Of course, this made me even more tense. Max came over asking what the problem was.

"Thumbthing's wrong," I quipped.

"I can't move his thumb," Doug said.

Suzanne faithfully chirped, "He's been a drag the whole morning."

Max looked at them. "How long have you been using his thumb?"

Neither of them answered.

"Are you positive he's rebelling against you?" Max continued.

Doug, picking up on Max's tack, mumbled, "Let's test your thumb."

Within minutes, he dialed in the problem. "You have the frequency of strep rheumaticus," he said.

"What's that?" I asked innocently, as if I didn't know, having seen it hundreds of times.

"It's the frequency of rheumatoid arthritis," he answered. "It makes the joints stiff."

"Particularly the thumbs," I said, quoting the standard.

Max turned to the two testers. "You've both committed the cardinal sin."

They waited for the axe to fall.

"You forgot to ask 'why,'" he told them.

"Let's get a new thumb," Doug said. "We've used him up."

"I'm calling my attorney," I threatened.

*   *   *

A woman phoned Max in desperation, saying her marriage was threatened. Her husband had just bought her a new BMW and she claimed she was allergic to it.

"But," she continued, "I'm allergic to everything. I'm a universal reactor."

Max explained that he could not test for the frequencies of BMWs as opposed to Chevrolets. But he could see what substances indicated a frequency of allergic reaction for her. Evaluation for allergy frequencies was routine.

When we tested, she appeared to be correct. She was allergic to *everything*. The BMW was easy. Max had owned several BMWs and the moment he saw she was reacting to the frequency of horsehair, he announced that he knew what the problem was.

"Any upholstery shop could save her marriage," he said. "The seats are covered with a layer of horse hair."

Further testing revealed the cause of her hypersensitivities. She had the frequency of a hereditary disease in the mucus membranes of her nose.

"That particular hereditary frequency almost always underlies the universal reactor syndrome," Max explained.

Not long after the frequency was removed, the woman reported that she hadn't bothered with the upholstery shop because her sensitivity was gone.

"In fact," she said, "for the first time in my life, I can be in a room with someone wearing perfume. I may even buy some."

Max advised her against it: "Have some consideration for universal reactors who don't know about Sanctuary. Or, even more important, people who can't stand the smell."

He hated perfume.

"The problem with allergies and energetic testing," Max explained to me, later, "is that you can't find an allergic frequency unless it's happening at that time. If she had been driving a Chevy, I would never have found the horsehair. If you don't eat tomatoes, you're not going to show the frequency of a tomato allergy, if you have one, because it's not happening. It's an example of 'It ain't broke, so you *can't* fix it.' When someone comes to me and says that every time they drink wine they get all stuffed up, I tell them to go have a glass of wine and come back. You'd be surprised how many people say they wouldn't dream of drinking wine in the morning. They think I'm decadent."

* * *

In accordance with the usual practice at Sanctuary, each member was called after a remote evaluation, so that they knew they had been checked and were being appropriately balanced. They weren't told which frequencies they manifested, though, because Max's position was that the names of the frequencies didn't matter; there was simply some kind of imbalance which was being corrected.

He would sometimes divulge that, "The frequencies we found might manifest as indigestion," or something to that effect, and perhaps tell them how long they might expect the imbalance to persist.

Normally, Sanctuary members were perfectly content with that. Occasionally a problem arose when the information was shared with someone who was both ignorant of and hostile toward the concept of energetic balancing. On one occasion, a member's doctor called, insisting that he be told what diseases were found.

Max took the call. "We didn't find any diseases," he told the doctor. "We never do."

"My patient had the symptoms of a respiratory disease and now they've cleared up. I need to know what that disease was." He coughed and Max waited for him to finish before replying.

"If your patient's symptoms are gone," Max said, "then whatever you did must have worked. Congratulations."

"But he refused to take my antibiotics," the doctor pushed.

"Then he must have healed himself," Max said. "Or perhaps you're a healer and don't know it."

"But what did I heal?"

"I don't know. What I *do* know is that your patient showed a subtle-energy frequency we identify as 1CE154, but he no longer shows that frequency."

"I've never heard of this 1CE154," the doctor said.

"That's because it's proprietary energetic information, not a disease," Max told him. "You don't deal in frequencies and I don't deal in diseases."

"Can I catch this 1CE-whatever?"

"Anyone can. It's quite common."

"Then what do I do about it?" The doctor's voice reflected his frustration.

"Have an energetic evaluation," Max answered calmly. He explained what an evaluation was.

The doctor sounded livid. "That's preposterous."

"I know," said Max. "I suggest you tell your patient that you spoke with me and I'm obviously a lunatic."

'You can rest assured that's exactly what I'll do."

Max hesitated and then said, "Doctor, are you aware that, according to the *British Medical Journal* of a hundred years ago, physicians seriously believed that if a menstruating woman touched a ham it would turn rancid?"

"That's absurd," he replied.

"I agree with you," Max said, "and, to be perfectly fair, there are many physicians today who share our enlightened view. But doesn't it make you wonder how your current beliefs and knowledge will stand up a hundred years from today?"

The phone went dead in Max's hand.

Max turned to me. "I find it's best to discourage people who are obviously not open to energetics," he said. "It saves time."

*   *   *

Max shook me out of a sound sleep. "We've got an emergency at the orphanage," he said.

I knew Max had always done a fair amount of charity work, without publicity. One of the local beneficiaries was a nearby home for orphaned Indian children. One of the children was violently ill. The onset had been very sudden. Within thirty minutes, the child had gone from quietly watching television to screaming in pain. The attending MD was at a loss for an explanation, but feared for the boy's life. His symptoms were severe and seemed to be increasing in intensity.

Sanctuary and its team of testers had already done regular energetic work with these children, primarily for emotional balance. The director of the orphanage suggested calling Sanctuary, but at first the MD refused. Finally, in the early morning, he capitulated.

I dressed quickly and stumbled down to Max's office. He was waiting for me, a faxed picture already on the testing plate. We began testing. And testing. The hits never seemed to stop.

Finally, more than twenty imbalances later, Max said, "Let's see what did this."

The screen showed the frequency of "Insect Vector." Max paged to a tray of insect frequencies and narrowed it down to "Spider."

"Amazing," he said. "All these frequencies from one bite."

The list of frequencies included those for yersinia pestis (commonly known as "the plague"), Western equine encephalitis, Rocky Mountain spotted fever, trench fever, Q fever, murine typhus, scrub typhus, rickettsial pox, tularemia and erlichosis, as well as three other frequencies which Max had discovered.

"This kid has all of these diseases at once?" It was hard to believe.

"Absolutely not," Max said. "He has these *frequencies.* It may not be conceivable that one spider could carry all these diseases, but it's highly possible for a spider to transmit the frequencies associated with all those diseases. It's like a complex harmonic travelling on a carrier wave. You keep forgetting, and I've got to keep reminding you, that the frequency is not the disease."

"Are these frequencies a danger to the other kids?" I asked.

"Not unless his frequency bites theirs," Max replied.

Max began imprinting the boy's picture. We monitored his progress periodically. Several hours later, every frequency was gone. Shortly after that, the director called back to report that the boy had no more fever or pain and the doctor said he was out of danger.

"Unfortunately," Max said, "it's likely they'll call back tomorrow with a new crisis."

"Because the boy might get bitten again?" I questioned.

"That's always possible, of course," he answered, "but it's more complicated than that. The problem with an insect bite is that it's an intrusion. It punches a hole in your energetic protective sheath, just like a leak in a roof, and whatever frequencies you are exposed to can easily gain a foothold from which to marshal their resources and attack. Commonly, the energetic results of a bite manifest themselves over the course of a couple of days. Let's see what else he's going to get."

He tested again, coming up with several more frequencies.

"What are you checking now?"

"Frequencies he's been exposed to," Max said, concentrating on the machine.

"Can you always do that?" I wondered. "And if you can, why don't you?"

"Of course I can do it," he acknowledged, "but it would be a futile, full-time job. If I followed Jennifer around while she did her Christmas shopping in a crowded closed-ventilation mall, I would spend the entire day finding new frequencies she is exposed to. What I'd need to know —

and currently can't know — is what frequencies she's *going to manifest*. But in the case of a *bite*, the frequencies are already inside. They're like eggs that are damn well going to hatch. One egg may take a day and another a week, but they're going to hatch. That's why I called it an intrusion."

Max had always railed against the dangers of insects. According to his tests, there was a huge list of frequency imbalances that came from their bites. Many of those were the frequencies associated with various "diseases of unknown etiology," i.e. no one knew how they were transmitted.

"Of course," Max commented, "there are no *frequencies* of unknown etiology."

*   *   *

We had a picture of a famous entertainer who called Max and said he was in concert that night in London and "would Max please take care of him." I stuck my thumb out, but Jennifer said it wasn't necessary.

She took the picture straight to an imprinter and entered some frequencies.

"All we have to do is fry the guy," she said.

I looked at what was on the screen of the imprinter. It made no sense to me.

"This frequency increases his vitality and stamina," Max explained. "Whereas this one improves his focus. This third frequency we found relaxes his throat so there's no tension in his voice. He hasn't given a concert in months without us being there."

"In spirit," Jennifer chimed in.

As it turned out, Max provided these frequencies, in addition to normal energetic balancing regimens, to many actors, actresses, singers, musicians, public speakers and others who wanted to perform at peak potential.

The next day, the performer called to thank Max, claiming that, once again, his concert was brilliant.

✳   ✳   ✳

One day Max received a visitor who was a prominent Catholic priest. Father Ernie solemnly handed Max two pictures — his mother and father — and asked Max to help resolve a "scriptural crisis."

"I believe *you're* the expert on the scriptures, Father," Max said.

"It's about the hereditary venereal frequency you found in me."

"It's gone," Max answered, "but I can't straighten your teeth."

"No, no," Father Ernie answered. "I need to know how long, how many generations I have had this. It may seem silly or unimportant to you, but it matters to me."

I had met Father Ernie before. He and Max had often discussed theology and the energy of faith. I knew they respected and admired each other.

Max began checking, using Father Ernie's thumb. First, he checked the mother, then the father. Then he kept checking further and further back. And finally said, "It goes back five generations, Father Ernie." Max showed him how he traced it back to a male ancestor who had acquired it, rather than inherited it as his descendants had.

"Thank God," the priest replied. "In the scriptures it says 'the sins of the fathers shall be visited upon their sons for seven generations.' If your machine had said it was *more* than seven..." He hesitated. "You know how much I love your work, Max, but my work is based on the Bible."

Max laughed and said, "Don't worry, Father, we're both under the line."

That afternoon, I wandered into the kitchen to find Father Ernie drinking coffee and chatting with Jennifer. I sat around awkwardly until he turned to me and said, "You look like a man with a question. Anything I can answer?"

"Yes there is," I replied. "You'll have to forgive me, but I'm kind of surprised to see a man of the cloth here at Sanctuary."

"We're allowed here," he smiled.

"Of course, but..."

"Let me help you," he offered. "You feel Sanctuary may be incompatible with my religion, is that it?"

"Well," I began, "*I* don't think so, but I thought that you might be uncomfortable with a religion based on consciousness, rather than the concept of 'salvation.'"

"Every religion is based on consciousness," he said, confidently, "and salvation is impossible without it. That is not where Max and I differ. I believe all consciousness is Christ Consciousness. Max, on the other hand, doesn't use my terminology."

"Isn't that a fundamental philosophical difference?" I asked.

"Not really," Ernie said. "We both believe all consciousness is of divine origin and the quest for consciousness is actually our need to reunite with our maker, the source of divinity."

I nodded.

Ernie winked. "I've just got to teach Max to be more precise with his language."

"Max is pretty strong-minded," I told him.

He smiled. "In my job, patience is a required virtue."

I still didn't understand how he resolved his faith with Max's work.

"Simply put, I believe in the healing power of prayer, both in the way I was taught to pray and in the way it is done here at Sanctuary," Father Ernie said. "Sanctuary is a religion — but one which coexists peacefully with my own. I am comfortable believing in the possibility of healing with Max's form of a prayer wheel, without feeling that my faith, which is the core of my life, is at all threatened. What Max does is a non-secular form of prayer, as far as I can tell, the purpose of which is *healing*. That word, as you may know, comes from the root 'whole' as in 'to make whole.' And in my mind wholeness is about the removal of obstacles to the realization of that divine spark within us."

Later that night, after Father Ernie had left, one of the testers questioned his biblical perspective. "This 'seven generations' thing — it seems a bit... superstitious."

Max turned to her and said, "Who are you to discount a wisdom based on thousands of years of knowledge, belief and understanding? Conceivably he's right. Can *you* prove otherwise?"

"What if it turned out to be eight generations?" I interjected.

"Curiously enough," Max answered, "I've never seen eight generations. And I've checked thousands of people."

One of the testers whistled a bar from the Twilight Zone theme and snickered.

Max spun around. "Your cynicism" he said sternly, "is inappropriate. Who are you to decide there is no spirit and that faith has no power or foundation? As a matter of fact, Father Ernie's faith is based upon something real. No one intelligent or evolved would ever discount ancient wisdom. Whatever survives thousands of years is based on collective knowledge and very well may be divinely inspired. I respect it and I suggest all of you do so as well — until you can disprove it. And you won't do it with cynicism.

"You may have noticed," Max said, "that people of many faiths have joined Sanctuary without abandoning their own faith. In fact, you're missing the point: It is those of great faith who have the most intuitive understanding of my work. They believe in information, they believe in energy and they believe in knowledge — whether or not those things exist in a world which is materially measurable. *As do we.* To suggest that someone abandon his faith because of my work, would be to diminish his life force, and, as a matter of fact, *yours.* Because faith *is* energy, positive energy, a form of sustenance. Religious teachings and beliefs, in my opinion, are always about energy in the infinite forms it takes. You must have belief, faith and passion to travel the path to consciousness. So I respect those beliefs and welcome those whose lives are enriched by them."

My Turn

EVERYTHING I HAD done in pursuit of energetic perfection came about because I was not satisfied with my physical, mental or emotional state. In short, I didn't feel good. And deep inside, I knew something better was possible. Fortunately, the path I chose — the path I stumbled into — proved that my perceptions were correct. In time I found that my mind, my body and my spirit were one and the same and they flourished together as my energetic balance improved.

An ongoing energetic regimen Max had worked on with me concerned frequencies in my pineal gland, a subtle organ reputed to be the connection between mind, body and spirit. He worked with frequencies that would activate and energize that gland. Over time, I began to notice the effects.

Initially, I didn't like being a thumb because I was primarily interested in me. The problems of others were not that important. As the energetic work on my pineal progressed, as measured by Max's testing, I became more and more involved in, and more and more sympathetic to the people we were evaluating. I'd begun to feel bonded to them and no longer cared about sitting on one side of the table or the other. I was just glad to be of help. Each morning, I couldn't wait to go in, stick out my thumb and see what was happening and I took a joy in seeing their negative frequencies reversed.

One night when Max and I were talking, I brought this up.

He smiled and said, "Good. Now it's time to use your other nine fingers. You're finished being a thumb."

"But I love doing this," I said. "There's still so much to learn."

"And there always will be," Max said. "We're like the astronomers looking through the Hubbell Space Telescope. They point it at the dark spots in the heavens and wait for them to resolve. And it always turns out that in the darkness there are still more stars and galaxies. There will always be more to learn, for all of us. But now it's time for you to start teaching."

"Teach who? How?"

"Everyone. Your field is communication, isn't it?" he replied.

"It used to be," I answered.

"It still is," said Max. "But you've gone beyond selling tuna fish and toilet paper. Take everything you've learned, including your recently-developed ability to care, and write about it. Write a book that will tell people what Sanctuary is and why each person needs it."

As I reflected on what I might say about what I'd experienced, Max said, gently, "It's time for you to leave Sanctuary."

"Leave Sanctuary?! It's become the center of my life."

"Leave *this* Sanctuary," he elaborated. "Because it's your job to make Sanctuary available everywhere. You can come back here if you insist, but you already know that it's not about a geographic location. The energetic work that people need can be done on anyone, anywhere. I need you to help me create a new Sanctuary. One without boundaries. And I feel you're ready to do it."

Max pulled out a bottle of tequila and we sat quietly, enjoying a parting drink together.

"This is where I came in," I said, raising my glass.

I knew it was a ritual we would repeat in another Sanctuary, soon.

*   *   *

I returned to the city and worked my way through the vast amount of notes I had taken. Periodically, I conferred with Max. He pointed me in the direction of an extensive literature dealing with scientific and mystical theory related to the energetic work he did.

We are in a time in which it is clear that legitimate science, when practiced with intellectual honesty, is a form of religious striving in mankind. The esoteric work of physicists and psychologists and philosophers explore the same terrain as mystics have throughout time. Max's work brings together many of these disciplines into a new branch of knowledge. But it is a branch which, like all the others, grows from the root of untapped human potential.

I and many other people have already worked through years of energetic balancing regimens. All of us have improved and evolved along with the improvements and evolutions in this unique system of knowledge. For myself, I have experienced time and again the usefulness of this regimen.

Little by little, throughout the process of the energetic work I have undergone, I have simultaneously undergone a personal awakening. I was dragged to this, kicking and screaming. At first, I had to expand my awareness to include the possibilities of well-being that Max had showed me. But even after years of energetic work, my reaction, upon first being introduced to the use of photographs for evaluation and imprinting, was a classic case of cognitive dissonance, a state in which intellectual comprehension completely conflicts with direct experience. Nonetheless, Max's demonstrations quickly convinced me, and the ensuing time has proven repeatedly that this method of applied energetics is as effective as, and much more convenient than, in-person evaluation.

My physical well-being has improved immensely over the time I have worked with energetic balancing. I have already recorded many specific examples of my experience and the experiences of others. But the more etheric results of this work may have even greater importance.

After telling Max that I had never been able to meditate, he found an energetic imbalance in my heart, associated with a condition that acupuncturists call "Restless Shen." Once this frequency was removed, I was able to meditate easily. At a more prosaic level, I also slept more deeply, without waking up in the middle of the night.

Perhaps most difficult to explain are my experiences related to work Max did on key energetic centers. These centers have long been associated with the endocrine system, which has been reputed to be the key to spiritual development. As Max found and removed imbalances in each energetic glandular center — thyroid, thymus, pancreas, adrenals, hypothalamus, pineal —. I began to shed limiting patterns. These patterns included such things as a need to be accepted by others and a complementary inability to receive their acceptance. Even more importantly, I developed an ability to accept myself, overcoming a disability I couldn't even perceive until it was gone.

When I discussed this with Max, he pointed out that these limitations have been chronicled throughout history.

"Linear thinking and mistrust of anything other than rationalism is a product of fear and ignorance," he said. "This has been true for thousands of years, as evidenced by Plato castigating his countrymen for believing only in that which can be seen. Today, most of us, like the people of Plato's time, are still trapped in the prison of our own limited perceptions, even though we currently use invisible powers such as electricity and magnetics every day of our lives."

As I've spoken to others about Max's work, I've listened to much skepticism and disbelief from the uninitiated. A common objection that comes up is that if the energetic world view is real, then hundreds of years of scientific knowledge would be wrong.

"It's not wrong," Max would say. "It's just another step in the continuum. And there will be more beyond what I have done. Because *we* can always be more. We *must* be. And we *must* always demand that."

We are living in a time when millions of people are opening themselves to greater possibilities than mere rationalism and materialism will allow. We see evidence of it in the books we read, the words we use, the way we live. Our time has greater possibilities for both growth and destruction than any other time in history. We are open to both, and only our consciousness can protect us. In every field of human knowledge and endeavor, leading thinkers are acknowledging the influence of consciousness and energy. But it is in Sanctuary where we have the opportunity to experience these ideas, not as abstract theories, but as practical and essential realities which can be applied — no, which *must* be applied — in our daily lives.

There is no need to "go gentle into that good night," reconciling ourselves to the inevitability of aging and the loss of vitality. Traditional Eastern cultures pursued longevity, not from a fear of death which is inconsistent with a belief in reincarnation, but because they desired to maximize the time available to perfect themselves in *this* life and therefore allow themselves the opportunity to live their lives free from the burden of the unwanted baggage which they called karma.

This is the real goal of Sanctuary and its work: To help each of us consciously unite with that divine energy which is in all things, of which all things are made — the continuum of energy which is our "self," without end. The mystery of the universe is that it is one continuous field of energy without boundaries and we ourselves are not only *part* of the mystery, we are *inextricable* from it. After all, what is consciousness? It is an absolute, it is a perfection you will never fully attain, only approach more and more closely. There is a vast body of cosmic information, the accumulation of all possible information — called by some the akashic records but it is known by many names. You already know *all* this information but are unaware of your knowing. Deep inside yourself, you know about *everything*. People you've never met, places you've never been, which nonetheless you know, infallibly. It is your life's purpose to bring that knowledge to a conscious level and my life's work to help guide you to that level. We speak of fully conscious beings as divinities. Rightly so. That's the reason we emulate them. Our task, the true task of integration and realization, is to become one with that which is already us, which is to say, become one with all things.

The accelerated timeline that we see in the computer industry, affectionately called "Netscape years," isn't something peculiar to the field of technology. All of us feel the stress of rapid change in every aspect of our lives. It is part of the zeitgeist. We all need to be able to respond rapidly to changes in our environment. In the same vein, our rapid evolution as energetic beings is essential to our survival. The tools are here and, once you know about them, there is no excuse for not using them. It becomes a responsibility for which you can no longer plead innocence.

As Bob Dylan said: "The times they are a'changin'."

Jane—
A Postscript

TWO YEARS LATER, Jane was at a cocktail party. She turned and saw a vaguely familiar face.

Acknowledging his look, she smiled and said, "Hello, George."

He looked flustered, trying to place her, then finally said, "I know you, but I can't quite..."

"It's Jane, Dr. Walker," she said. "I was a patient of yours."

His face registered several types of confusion. "Of course, Jane," he blurted. "I remember, but..."

"How come I'm not dead, George?"

"No, I'm thrilled, of course, it's just that... you didn't come back... I assumed you'd given up." He paused, awkwardly. "What did you do?"

"I used my own energy, George," she said. "Anyone can do it."

"Energy is well and good," said George, "and I approve of it. But you had cancer. I saw it, I showed it to you."

"Cancer is energy, too, George. It's just the wrong kind."

"You did a few courses of chemotherapy as I recall," he said. "Sometimes it takes a while for them to take effect."

"That must have been it." She extended her hand and said, "Well, thank you for all your help, George. Keep up the good work."

She turned and walked away.

"Jane —" he said.

She turned.

"This energy... the thing is..." he hesitated. "My wife has... an inoperable malignancy."

"I'm sorry, George."

"She talked to me about energy, too. Something about a sanctuary. And of course I forbade her."

"Why is that, George?"

"Well, consider my work," he said. "It would be humiliating, a slap in the face."

"You mean you'd be embarrassed?" she asked.

"Exactly," he asserted.

"Well then, George," she replied, "she won't be the first person to die of embarrassment. Actually, it's a rather common cause of death."

"You're both insulting and irrational," George barked, his face turning red.

"Yes, but I'm alive," she said. "Or perhaps you disagree with that also."

This time when she left, he did not call her back.

An Invitation

TO SUPPORT THIS WORK of the energetic integration of mind, body and spirit, Sanctuary: the Energetic Matrix Church of Consciousness (EMC^2) was formed. The energetic work illustrated in this book may be available to you via this organization. Because EMC^2 is based upon belief in the eternal and energetic nature of all things, we welcome members of other faiths and support the continuation of their existing spiritual practices, beliefs and memberships.

If you want information about how you may receive energetic balancing, contact us at:

EMC^2
626 Santa Monica Boulevard, Suite 547
Santa Monica, CA 90401-2538

toll-free: 877-500-EMCC
World-Wide Web: http://www.matrixchurch.com

Annotated Contents

Index

["